ABUSED, CONFUSED & MISUSED WORDS

A WRITER'S GUIDE TO USAGE, SPELLING, GRAMMAR, AND SENTENCE STRUCTURE

MARY EMBREE

Skyhorse Publishing

Skyhorse Publishing books may be purchased in bulk at special discounts for sales promotion, corporate gifts, fund-raising, or educational purposes. Special editions can also be created to specifications. For details, contact the Special Sales Department, Skyhorse Publishing, 307 West 36th Street, 11th Floor, New York, NY 10018 or info@skyhorsepublishing.com.

Skyhorse® and Skyhorse Publishing® are registered trademarks of Skyhorse Publishing, Inc.®, a Delaware corporation.

Visit our website at www.skyhorsepublishing.com.

10 9 8 7 6 5 4 3 2 1

Interior design by Robin Black
Page composition/typography by Integra Software Services, Pvt. Ltd., Pondicherry, India

Library of Congress Cataloging-in-Publication Data is available on file.
ISBN: 978-1-62087-047-1

Printed in China

This book is dedicated to

MY GRANDSON ALEXANDER FLEISCHER *who,*

at almost 2, is falling in love with words.

Contents

Introduction

A word fitly spoken is like apples of gold in pictures of silver.

—PROVERBS 25:11

Is it any wonder that words are abused, confused, and misused so often when language is so incredibly complex and it comes in so many forms? Whether we're teaching, conducting business, or having a personal conversation, using appropriate words is essential for clarity. Words have the power to ignite anger, inflame passions, and destroy relationships. But they also have the power to pacify, console, educate, amuse, and express love.

There are many different languages in the world, which means that we do not have a common base of words to work with. The wide variations of meaning in our vocabularies create the challenge of communicating clearly with people whose language is not the only dividing factor. Their culture, philosophy, and belief systems are not like our own. Ludwig Wittgenstein said, "If we spoke a different language, we would perceive a somewhat different world." He also said, "The limits of my language mean the limits of my world." Using an inappropriate word can cause misunderstandings, and misunderstandings can have serious consequences.

If we want to reach our audience, we need to simplify our language and adapt our words to our readers' repertoire. Simplification also makes for better writing. The German philosopher Arthur Schopenhauer said, "Writers should use common words to say uncommon things."

When computers and the Internet became a major part of our everyday lives, communication moved into the fast lane. We no longer have time to waste addressing and stamping envelopes. E-mail has become a quick way to communicate and, as we dash off messages, we tend to get sloppy. Sometimes we don't take the time to punctuate, capitalize, or spell correctly, let alone use words properly. Even though we're all so busy, I believe it is still important to be concerned about the quality of our writing. To quote Samuel Johnson, English author and lexicographer, "What is written without effort is in general read without pleasure!"

The ability to speak and write well is valued in practically every field and in most business and personal relationships. This book is intended to help you say what you really mean.

Chapter One

Word Usage

Proper words in proper places,
make the true definition of a style.

—JONATHAN SWIFT [1667–1745]

IF YOU LOVE WORDS, you probably like to read a wide variety of things: novels, nonfiction books, newspapers, magazines, comic books, cereal boxes. If you read a lot, you probably write pretty well because you've seen a lot of writing and have noticed how writers put sentences together. You've seen how words are commonly spelled and observed that most writing has a pattern to it. Most likely, you appreciate the beauty of communicating through the amazing versatility of words and want to use them to the best of your ability yourself.

The artistry of words can pull us inside a story, making us feel what the characters feel. A great novel can carry us off into another dimension, into a fantasy so engrossing that we forget all our earthly cares. A magnificent book is almost orgasmic. We want it to go on and on.

Word appreciation is similar to music appreciation. The more we learn about words and music, the more we enjoy them in all of their forms: from magazines to novels, from popular music to classical. Whether it's words or music, it is communication and I believe that the better we are at it, the happier we will be. As Alexander Pope said, "True ease in writing comes from art, not chance, as those move easiest who have learned to dance."

Learning to write well is not so different from learning to dance well. It is much more fun when we learn the steps. Although we were taught the basics in school and have been writing most of our lives, sometimes it helps to be reminded of some of the "steps" involved in expressing ourselves through words.

Because communication can be formal or informal, the setting or field in which one is working generally determines its nature. Formal writing is usually used for scientific and scholarly papers, technical and business reports, and legal briefs, to name just a few. Those cases call for the current professionally accepted rules of writing.

Informal writing is more suitable for commercial messages, scripts, poetry, novels, personal letters, notes, e-mail, and many other types of written communication. In such everyday writing, we might want to relax the rules a little and write more from our hearts than from our heads. That doesn't mean that we needn't be concerned with spelling and sentence structure at all. Our written communications are extensions of ourselves, which project an image of who we are. E-mail doesn't give us license to throw all the rules out the window. Business e-mail should be as well composed as a hard copy we send through the mail. Sloppy writing is okay only in very personal messages.

THE PARTS OF SPEECH

Whether writing is formal or informal, our ideas come across with greater clarity when we use words appropriately in a sentence. An incorrect word can change the meaning, sometimes drastically. Consider the frequently confused words *enervate* and *energize*. If you were to say, "His words enervate me," it would mean they make you tired. If you say they energize you, you would be saying that they give you vigor. These are opposite meanings.

Sentences have four purposes: to state, to question, to command, and to express surprise or other strong emotion (exclamatory). A sentence that *states* is called a declarative sentence. It makes a statement: *I am going to the movies.* A sentence that *asks* is an interrogative sentence: *Are you going to watch the games on TV all day?* A sentence that expresses a *command* is called an imperative sentence: *Get off that couch and come with me!* *That's outrageous!* is an example of an exclamatory sentence.

Words are classified according to their functions in sentences. It is generally agreed that there are eight parts of speech: nouns, pronouns, verbs, adjectives, adverbs, prepositions, conjunctions, and interjections.

There are also articles. The definite article is *the*. *The* specifies something or someone in particular: *The person you need to see is Mr. Jones. The cat is black and white.* Indefinite articles are *a* and *an*. *A* is used before words beginning with a consonant sound, and *an* is used before a vowel sound. So it's *a pear, a car, a child,* but it's *an orange, an automobile, an orphan.* Some vowels have a consonant sound and when they do you should use *a: a union, a European.* Some consonants have a vowel sound so you would use *an: an hour, an honest person, an herb.*

Nouns

A noun is a word that denotes a thing, place, person, quality, state, or action. It functions in a sentence as the subject or object of an action expressed by a verb. It can also be the object of a preposition. There are proper nouns and common nouns. Proper nouns denote individuals and personifications and are always capitalized: *Alice, Thomas, New York, The Associated Press.* In the sentence, *Tom is from Georgetown, back East,* the words *Tom, Georgetown,* and *East* are capitalized because they refer to a specific person and specific places. A general name common to all persons, places, or things is called a common noun. In modern English, common nouns are not capitalized: *girl, man, city, newspaper.* For example: *The boy's home is on the east side of town.*

There are concrete and abstract nouns. Anything physical that can be perceived by the senses is a concrete noun: *Some books are to be tasted, others to be swallowed* (Francis Bacon). An abstract noun is a quality, action, or idea which cannot be perceived by the senses: *A foolish consistency is the hobgoblin of little minds* (Ralph Waldo Emerson).

There are also collective nouns which name a group of individuals as though they were one: *jury, committee, family, flock, regiment.* And, depending on the purpose it serves, a collective noun can be either singular or plural. In the sentence, *The board was unanimous in its decision,* meaning it acted as one person, *board* is a singular form of the collective noun. In *The board were arguing over increasing membership dues,* the board members were acting as individuals so in this case the *board* is considered a plural noun.

Pronouns

A pronoun is an identifying word which substitutes for a noun. A pronoun can indicate a noun (such as a person's name) already mentioned to avoid repetition: *Charlie is the lead dancer; he is the tall one in the front row.* There are several kinds of pronouns: personal, demonstrative, indefinite, relative, interrogative, numerical, reflective, and reciprocal.

A personal pronoun indicates (1) the speaker, (2) the person spoken to, or (3) the person, place, or thing spoken about. The speaker is first person: *I, my* or *mine, me, we, our* or *ours, us.* The person spoken to is second person: *you, your, yours.* The person, place, or thing spoken about is third person: *he, she, it, they, his, her, hers, him, its, their, theirs, them.* Here is a sentence that contains all three forms of personal pronouns: *I loaned you my sweater but you gave it to her as a present.*

Demonstrative pronouns are *this, that, these,* and *those.* They indicate a person or thing specifically: *This is my sweater. That one is yours. These are my friends. Those are yours.*

Indefinite pronouns refer to people or things in general. Some indefinite pronouns are: *all, everybody, everything, anyone, another, many, more, several, either, neither, both, each.* An example of usage in a sentence is *Everybody loves somebody sometime.*

A relative pronoun plays two roles, both as a pronoun and as a connective. It is a subject or object in a subordinate part of a sentence, and it joins the subordinate to a more important part of a sentence. Relative pronouns are *who, which, that, what, whose,* and *whom.* Example: *He is the man whose footsteps I heard.* Some compound relative pronouns are *whoever, whosoever, whatever, whichever, whatsoever,* and *whomever.*

Interrogative pronouns help ask questions. They are *who, which, what, whom,* and *whose. Whose sweater is this? Which one of you borrowed it? Who will return it to me?*

Reflective pronouns are formed by adding *self* or *selves* to the personal pronoun. They are *myself, yourself, himself, herself, itself, ourselves, yourselves,* and *themselves.* This kind of pronoun can be used as an object referring to the same person as the subject: *She lives by herself.*

A reciprocal pronoun represents two or more people or things interchanging the action of the verb: *They love each other.*

Verbs

Verbs express an action, state of being, occurrence, or a relation between two things. Inflection or conjugation of a verb involves changes of form according to person and number, tense, voice (active and passive), and mood. Person and number refer to who and how many performed the action. Tense indicates the action performed. Present tense, for example, would be *know;* past tense would be *knew;* past participle would be *known. I know you can dance. I knew you danced. I have known for a long time that you could dance.* Voice indicates whether the subject of the verb performed (active) or received (passive) the action: *Jim kicked the ball* (active). *The ball was kicked by Jim* (passive). Mood indicates the frame of mind of the performer. Verbs have three moods: the indicative, which expresses actuality: *I dance*; the subjunctive, which expresses contingency: *I might dance*; and the imperative, which expresses command: *Dance!*

Adverbs

Adverbs modify verbs, adjectives, or other adverbs or adverbial phrases, clauses, and sentences, and alter their meaning in some way. For example, in the sentence *She moves slowly*, the adverb *slowly* modifies the verb *moves*. In *She moves in a very slow manner*, the adverb *very* modifies the adjective *slow*. In *She moves very slowly*, the adverb *very* modifies the adverb *slowly*. Adverbs may indicate place or direction (*where, there*), time (*today, tomorrow*), degree (*nearly, completely*), manner (*carefully, slowly*), belief or doubt (*surely, maybe*), and how often (*never, always*).

Adverbs are classified as simple or conjunctive depending on their use. A simple adverb alters the meaning of a single word. A conjunctive adverb modifies the sentence or clause it appears in.

Adjectives

An adjective modifies a noun or pronoun by limiting, qualifying, or describing it in one of three forms of degree: positive (*happy, beautiful*), comparative (*happier, more beautiful*), or superlative (*happiest, most beautiful*). Adjectives are distinguished by having endings like *-er* and *-est*, as in big, bigger, biggest. An adjective usually precedes the noun it directly modifies: *blue* dress, *heavy* book, *beautiful* child.

Prepositions

A preposition is a word that combines with a noun or pronoun to form a phrase. It expresses the relationship between words: *from* here *to* there; one *after* another; water *under* the bridge. Examples of prepositions are *to, through, in, into, for, on, at, with, about, along, after, before, during, between, among,* and *from*. In casual speech, it's no longer a crime to end a sentence with a preposition. It's now perfectly all right to say, *That's where she came from; He's the man she gave her heart to; They're the couple everybody is talking about.*

Conjunctions

Conjunctions, such as *and, or, but, though, if, unless, however,* and *because* connect sentences, clauses, phrases, or words. There are two kinds of conjunctions: coordinate and subordinate. Coordinate conjunctions join words, independent clauses, or parts of a sentence that are of the same rank or order: *Virtue is bold and goodness never fearful* (Shakespeare). Examples of these are *and, but, or, yet;* conjunctive adverbs *however, nevertheless;* and correlative conjunctions *neither/nor.* Subordinate conjunctions introduce subordinate clauses. *Where, when, after, while, if, unless, since, because, although,* and *whether* are subordinate conjunctions: *I will go when I am ready. He won't stay unless he's invited to dinner.* Subordinate conjunctions may also function as prepositions.

It is no longer considered wrong to begin a sentence with a conjunction. And I do that frequently.

Interjections

Interjections are usually used to express an emotional reaction: *Oh! Ow! Yipes! Hurrah!* They are also used for emphasis: *Aha!* The interjection has no grammatical relation to the other parts of the sentence.

There are a few other principles of word usage that are worthy of consideration, such as the following.

- In most cases, use the active rather than the passive voice: *I'd love for you to come to my party,* not *Your presence is requested.*
- Write clearly. Simplifying your writing is not dumbing it down. It is making it available to readers who don't want to struggle with trying to figure out what you mean. According to Walter Savage Landor, "Clear writers, like fountains, do not seem so deep as they are; the turbid look the most profound."
- Be concise. Long sentences and strings of polysyllabic words tend to muddy your meaning. Sprinkling a lot of arcane words throughout your writing makes it difficult for those with less than a genius IQ to read and understand. Not all authors agree with this principle. William Faulkner said of Ernest Hemingway, "He has never been known to use a word that might send a reader to the dictionary." Hemingway responded, "Poor Faulkner. Does he really think big emotions come from big words?"

■ Get rid of unnecessary words and avoid redundancies. Superfluous words are everywhere, on broadcast news, in newspapers and magazines, in movies and television. It's hard to understand why anyone needs to say *enter into an agreement*. You can't enter *out* of anything. And why say *dropped down* as though it were possible to drop *up*? Cops never make that mistake. It's much quicker to say, "Drop the gun!" Time is of the essence. There are so many other redundancies littering our language: *revert back, reiterate again, previous history*, and *follow behind*. If a word doesn't add information, why use it?

Because language is in a constant state of flux, common usage alters the meaning and proper usage of a word. So-called correct word usage is a temporary thing. When a word is so frequently misused that its meaning changes, its new usage becomes standard and it is no longer wrong.

We often think of a dictionary as an authority, but it doesn't dictate proper word usage. It is merely a guide to the current standard in word definitions. And, have you noticed, all dictionaries don't agree with each other regarding definitions?

Chapter Two

Old Rules, New Rules

Fashion, though folly's child, and guide of fools,
Rules e'en the wisest, and in learning rules.

—GEORGE CRABB [1754–1832]

THE TREND IN WORD USAGE is toward less formality. There is no longer a great distinction between the way one speaks and the way one writes. Both have become more casual. When people in the same profession such as law, medicine, psychology, or other fields communicate with each other, jargon is okay because they understand their specialized vocabulary. However, when they are writing or speaking to a layperson, it's best to use words that are familiar to the general public.

Over the past fifty years, Americans have become less formal in many ways. Rules about dress have become relaxed for both men and women. The rules of etiquette have become more relaxed, too. I have mixed feelings about the relaxation of the rules when it comes to language, yet I much prefer a casual style to a stilted, formal way of communicating. It puts the reader or listener at ease. And I really think it's a good thing that we no longer have to worry about ending a sentence with a preposition, or dangling a participle, or misplacing a modifier. What matters is that our meaning is clear.

Language changes constantly. So does spelling. So do the rules. It has been said, "rules are made to be broken." I don't know about that, but I do believe in letting go of the rules when they get in the way of what you want to say.

If you choose to break the rules, however, it is probably a good idea to know what the rules (and their exceptions) are so that you can make a conscious, educated decision about which ones to follow and which ones to ignore.

In gathering qualified, up-to-date material for this book, I have consulted several recently published dictionaries as well as *The Chicago Manual of Style*. Generally, they were in agreement as to word definitions and rules. When they differed, I chose the ones that seemed most logical to me.

Included in the following are some examples of changes that have occurred over the past thirty or forty years. You will find more of these rules and usage changes in the misused words list (chapter 4).

Who or Whom

The old rules stated that the choice of *who* or *whom* must be determined by the grammar of the clause within which this pronoun occurs. *Who* is the appropriate form for the subject of a sentence or clause: *Who is he? He's the man who wants the key. Whom* is the objective form: *Whom did he say he was? He's a man whom I know well.*

Those distinctions are rarely observed anymore. Because *who* or *whom* frequently occur at the beginning of a sentence or clause, there is a tendency to choose *who* no matter what the word's function is. According to *Webster's New Universal Unabridged Dictionary* (1996), "Even in edited prose, *who* occurs at least ten times as often as *whom* regardless of grammatical function. Only when it directly follows a preposition is *whom* more likely to occur than *who*." This juxtaposition is usually avoided now both in speech and writing, particularly in questions: *Who is the letter from?* Sometimes it's avoided by omitting the pronoun altogether: *All patients you have had contact with.*

The word *whom* has gone almost completely out of style. And good riddance. Most people use it incorrectly anyway. According to *Random House Webster's Unabridged Dictionary 3.0*, "The notion that 'whom' is somehow more 'correct' or elegant than 'who' leads some speakers to hypercorrect uses of 'whom': *Whom are you? The person whom is in charge of the office has left the building.*" That sounds so yesterday.

The new rules seem to indicate that it's best (and most natural) to use *whom* only after a preposition: *to whom it may concern; to whom are you speaking?* For formal writing, check your dictionary if you aren't sure when to use *whom* because there are still sticklers for the "proper" use of this practically archaic word and it's best to use it correctly. Your college English professor and certain periodicals, such as *TIME* magazine, will not accept the less formal *who* when *whom* is technically correct. However, if your main concern is clarity and you don't care who you impress, just use *who* and don't worry about it.

Absolutes

Certain words are absolutes, which means that they are complete, unconditional, and unqualifiable. Thus, according to many usage guides, one should not use comparison words with them. However, it's done all the time.

Perfect is a good example of an absolute. It means excellent or complete beyond practical or theoretical improvement. *Perfect* cannot exist in varying degrees. But since the thirteenth century, the word *perfect* has often been qualified: *the most perfect day we've had*. A famous misuse is in the United States Constitution: "in order to form a more perfect union."

Another absolute is the word *unique*. *Unique* means existing as the only one or as the sole example. How can something be very one-of-a-kind? When it first entered the English language in the 1600s, its meaning was single, sole, having no equal. *Unique* developed the wider meaning of not typical and unusual by the mid-nineteenth century. Some examples are: *He is more unique than anyone else* and *It was a very unique day*.

According to the dictionaries I checked, using so-called absolutes in senses that are not absolute has become standard in most forms of speech and writing. Even so, I still choose not to use qualifiers with absolutes because, once you do that, the word is no longer an absolute.

Old and New Plurals

The plurals of some words often depend on whether they are used in a scholarly work or in more casual writing. Examples of these (noting the informal word first) are *appendixes* and *appendices*, *memorandums* and *memoranda*, *millenniums* and *millennia*, *symposiums* and *symposia*. Most dictionaries list the less formal as the preferred usage. The same word may have different plurals depending on its definition. A book could have two *indexes* while a mathematical expression might have two *indices*.

None Is vs. None Are

Because *none* means "not one" and "not any," some believe that the word should always be treated as singular and followed by a singular verb. However, since the ninth century *none* has been used with both singular and plural verbs. When it is used to mean "not any," the plural verb is generally used: *We dove for coins but none were found*. When it is intended to mean "not one," it is followed by a singular verb: *In spite of all the prophecies, none has come true.* Currently, *none* is usually seen with a plural verb. So if you can't remember the subtle differences, you can use either a plural or a singular verb and probably no one will even notice—or care.

Each

The adjective *each* is always followed by a singular noun: *each person, each book.* When the adjective follows a plural subject, the verb agrees with the subject: *the children each have many books.* When the pronoun *each* comes immediately before the verb, it takes a singular verb: *Each lives in a different neighborhood.* When the pronoun is followed by a phrase containing a plural noun, the verb can be plural: *Each of them have lovely homes.*

Anyone, anybody, everyone, everybody, no one, someone, and somebody follow the same general patterns of pronoun agreement as *each* and *none.* However, these are not hard and fast rules anymore but guidelines for formal writing. For dialogue or other forms of casual writing, it is not necessary to concern yourself with these rules.

An Historical or A Historical

Is it *an historical study* or *a historical study?* The current rule is, if the *h* is pronounced, you use *a*; if it is not, you use *an*. So it's *a historical study*, but it's *an honor* and *an heir*. The same is true of a pronounced long *u* or *eu*: *a union, a euphemism*, and an *o* when it is pronounced like a *w*: a one-room house.

Different From or Different Than

Some believe that *different* should be followed only by *from* and never by *than*. But that is not the case, at least not anymore. *From* is more common in introducing a phrase: My opinions are different from yours. *Than* is used to introduce a clause: *The prisoner ran in a different direction than the bystanders indicated.* If you were to use *from* in a sentence like this, you would have to add a few words: *The prisoner ran in a different direction from the one that the bystanders indicated.*

If you find it hard to remember these distinctions, don't worry because this is another case where it really doesn't matter which word you use. No matter how the sentence is constructed, both *from* and *than* are now standard usage after *different*. In fact, both have been used for at least three hundred years. And that makes it okay.

That vs. Who

The general rule is: a person is a *who*; a thing is a *that*. You would say: *Is this the chair that has a broken leg?* and *Is he the man who has a broken leg?* An anonymous animal is a *that* but an animal with a name is a *who*. For example: *Was it Fifi who bit the mailman?* but *Was it a stray dog that bit the mailman?*

It has now become acceptable to use *that* when referring to a person. However, using *who* often helps the understanding of a sentence that contains both a person and a thing. It makes it easier to understand to whom (or to which) you are referring.

Compare To or Compare With

Compare means to examine two or more things in order to note similarities and differences: *to compare two styles of shoes. Compare* should be followed by *to* when it points out similarities between two apparently dissimilar things: *He compared her hairdo to a string mop.*

Compare should be followed by *with* when it points out similarities or differences between two entities of the same general class: *The diner compared the crème brûlée with custard pudding.*

This is another rule that is so frequently broken that it doesn't really matter anymore whether you use *compare to* or *compare with.*

A few words about punctuation. It is not possible to cover all instances of proper punctuation so I'll cover only a few of the more frequent challenges. Most writers overuse commas, sprinkling them all over their manuscripts like confetti. The modern trend is to use as few commas as you can without muddying the meaning of a sentence. We no longer write: *My sister, Alice, looks great in red.* Instead it is: *My sister Alice looks great in red.* No commas are needed in that sentence for it to be clear.

According to *The Chicago Manual of Style,* "In a series consisting of three or more elements, the elements are separated by commas. When a conjunction joins the last two elements in a series, a comma is used before the conjunction." Example: *Would you like coffee, tea, milk, or hot chocolate?*

Before computers, we used to space twice after the period at the end of a sentence. But that was way back when we used typewriters (remember those?). Separating sentences with two spaces is no longer necessary because computers space the text more uniformly. Now we hit the space bar only once between sentences.

In American English, periods and commas are placed inside quotation marks.

Colons are used to introduce a statement, as in: *The rule is this: Lights out at 10 p.m., period!* A colon is also used to introduce a speech in dialogue:

MARY: May I introduce my friend?

JOHN: We've already met.

A colon should go outside quotation marks and parentheses. *There are two reasons not to take a small child to see the movie "Babel": it is violent and it is very disturbing. I was concerned about one of the girls standing in the hot sun (the blonde): she looked like she was going to faint.*

Semicolons are used less frequently than in the past. The current practice is to use a comma if it's a brief pause. Otherwise, use a period. In a series where each item includes a comma, a semicolon is used to separate them. For example: *Those who attended the meeting were Sam Cooke, President; Richard Jones, Secretary; and Alice Smith, Treasurer.*

A semicolon should be placed outside quotation marks or parentheses.

Exclamation points are to be used very sparingly. Here are two examples of when not to use one: *"What a game!" he exclaimed,* and, *"I was absolutely astounded!"* With these kinds of sentences, an exclamation point is redundant. If the sentence is written so that the emphasis is clear, no exclamation point is necessary. In her bestselling book, *Eats, Shoots & Leaves,* Lynn Truss writes that "in humorous writing, the exclamation mark is the equivalent of canned laughter."

Place the exclamation point inside quotation marks, parentheses, or brackets when it is part of the quotation or parenthetical expression. Otherwise, place it outside.

Question marks aren't always at the end of a sentence and can be used to indicate a question within a sentence, such as: *Is he looking at me? she wondered.* Place a question mark inside quotation marks, parentheses, or brackets when it belongs to the quoted or parenthetical matter.

British and American punctuation rules are not the same. For example, in the United States, a period always goes inside quotation marks. In England, it depends on the sentence. In fact, they don't seem to have a hard and fast rule for that.

British English is also different from American English when it comes to word usage, spelling, and many other things. Some of the same words and phrases have entirely different meanings. In England, *knock up* means to wake up or call; in America, it means to make pregnant.

The most comprehensive publishing reference work, of course, is *The Chicago Manual of Style.* I recommend that you use it as your authority when you write.

Chapter Three

Word Roots

Burrow awhile and build, broad on the roots of things.

—ROBERT BROWNING [1812–1889]

A BASIC UNDERSTANDING OF WORD ROOTS, prefixes, and suffixes may help you with the meaning of a word. For example, many people make the mistake of saying *hyperdermic* when they mean *hypodermic*. When you know that the prefix *hypo* means *under,* it becomes very clear that a needle that goes under the skin is called a *hypodermic needle.*

Most prefixes and suffixes are from Greek or Latin words. For example, the prefix *biblio* is based on a Greek word meaning "book" or "Bible." The suffix *phobe* is derived from the Greek word *phōbos,* which means "fear" or "panic." Thus, a *bibliophobe* is someone who is afraid of books or, perhaps, of the Bible.

Many words have been coined by combining a prefix with a suffix, or by combining a prefix or suffix with another word from a language other than Greek or Latin.

Unfortunately, you can't depend on a particular prefix to always mean the same thing. The same is true of the suffix. Usually the prefix *in-* means "not." But not always. Both *flammable* and *inflammable* mean "combustible" even though it would make sense to expect *inflammable* to mean "*not* flammable." Both *genius* and *ingenious* mean "brilliant," and both *valuable* and *invaluable* mean "of great value or importance."

The following is a list of common word roots.

Word Roots

a	not, from: *asexual; atheist*
ab	away, from: *abnormal; abduct*
acantho	thorn: *acanthoid*
aceto	acid, vinegar: *acetone*
acous	hearing: *acoustic*
acro	top, tip, summit, height: *acrophobia*
ad	to, toward: *advent; adverse*
adeno	gland: *adenoma*
aero	air, gas: *aerobatics; aerosol*
agri	field: *agriculture*
algia	pain: *neuralgia*
allo	other, different: *allonym*
alti, alto	high: *altimeter; altostratus*
ambi	both: *ambidextrous; ambivalence*
amphi	both, on both sides, around: *amphibious; amphitheater*
amylo	starch: *amyloid*
an	not, without: *anhydrous*
andro	man, masculine: *androgen*
androus	man: *polyandrous*
anemo	wind: *anemometer*
ante	before: *antecedent*
anthrop	human being: *anthropomorphism*
anti	against: *antichrist; antiestablishment*
api	bee: *apiary*
apo	away from, separate, without: *apogee; apodal; apothem*
aqua, aqui	water: *aquafarm; aquiculture*
arbori	tree: *arborization*
arch	principal: *archenemy*; prototypical: *archetype*; chief, leader, ruler: *monarch; matriarch*
archae	old, ancient: *archaeology*
archy	rule, government: *monarchy; oligarchy*
arthro	joint: *arthroscopy*
aster, astro	star: *asteroid; astrophysics*
atmo	vapor: *atmosphere*
audio	hearing: *audiotape*

auto	self: *autobiography, autograph*
avi	bird: *aviculture*
bacci	berry: *bacciferous*
baro	weight: *barometer*
batho, bathy	deep: *bathometer; bathysphere*
belli	war: *bellicose; rebellion*
bene	good: *benefit*; well: *benediction*
bi	two: *bicycle*
biblio	book: *bibliography*
bio	life: *biography; biopsy*
biosis	life: *aerobiosis; parabiosis*
blast	bud: *ectoblast*
blepharo	eyelid: *blepharospasm*
brevi	short: *brevity*
broncho	windpipe: *bronchoscope*
caco	bad: *cacophony*
calc	lime or calcium: *calcify*
cardio	heart: *cardiogram*
carp	fruit: *apocarpous*
cata/cath	down, through: *catalog; catheter*
cede	go: *precede*
cele	tumor: *blastocele*
centi	hundred: *centimeter*
cephalo	head: *cephalopod*
cerebro	brain: *cerebrovascular*
cero	wax: *cerography*
chiro	hand: *chirography*
chloro	green: *chlorophyll*
chole	bile: *cholera*
chore	dance: *choreography*
chromato	color: *chromatolysis; chromatography*
chrome	color: *polychrome*
chrono	time: *chronological*
cidal, cide	kill: *suicidal; homicide*
circum	around: *circumference; circumnavigate*
cirro	cloud: *cirrostratus*
cis	near, on the near side of: *cisatlantic*
clino	slope: *clinometer*

coccus	spherical bacterium: *streptococcus*
col, com, con	with, together, in association: *collaboration; combine; convene*
contra	against: *contradictory*
cosmo	universe: *cosmonaut*
cracy, crat	rule, government: *democracy, plutocrat*
cranio	skull: *craniotomy*
cruci	cross: *crucify*
cryo	cold: *cryogenics*
crypto	hidden: *cryptogram*
cysto	bladder: *cystotomy*
cyto	cell: *cytoplasm*
dactylo	finger, toe: *dactylography*
de	not, down: *decompress; descent*
deca	ten: *decade*
deci	tenth: *decibel*
demi	half: *demigod*
demo	people: *democratic; demography*
dendro	tree: *dendroid*
denti	tooth: *dentifrice*
dermo	skin: *dermoplasty*
dia	through: *diameter*
diction	speech: *contradiction*
digit	finger: *digitate; prestidigitation*
dino	terrible: *dinosaur*
dis	apart: *dislocate; disbar*
dorso	back (of body): *dorsolumbar*
dyna	force, power: *dynamite*
dys	evil, difficult: *dysfunction*
echino	spiny: *echinoderm*
ecto	outside, external: *ectomorph*
emia	blood: *anemia*
en	in, into: *energy*
encephalo	brain: *encephalogram*
endo	within: *endoscopy; endocardial*
entero	gut: *enterology*
ento	inside, interior: *entoderm*
entomo	insect: *entomology*

eo	dawn, early: *Eocene*
eph	on: *ephedrine*
epi	over: *epitome*
equi	equal: *equidistant*
ergo	work: *ergograph*
erythro	red: *erythrocyte*
ethno	race, culture, people: *ethnography*
eu	happiness, well-being: *eudemonia; euphoria*
ex	out: *ex-member*
exo	outside, external: *exocentric*
extra	outside, external: *extracurricular*
factor	maker, doer: *benefactor*
febri	fever: *febrific*
ferri	iron: *ferriferous*
fication	making: *deification; pacification; beautification*
fid	divided: *bifid*
fissi	cleft, split: *fissiparous; fission*
fluvi	river: *fluvial*
fuge	away from: *centrifuge*
galacto	milk: *galactometer*
gamo	joined, united: *gamogenesis*
gamy	marriage: *bigamy*
gastro	stomach: *gastronomy*
gemmi	bud: *gemmiform*
geny	origin: *progeny*
geo	earth, land: *geography*
geronto	old age: *gerontology*
gnathous	jaw: *prognathous*
gnomy, gnosis	knowledge: *physiognomy*
gon	angle: *pentagon*
gonium	seed: *archegonium*
grade	walking: *plantigrade*
gram, graph	writing: *epigram; lithograph*
glosso	tongue: *glossolalia*
glyco	sweet: *glycolipid*
glyph	carving: *hieroglyph*
gnathous	jaw: *prognathous*
gono	reproduction (sexual): *gonophore*

grapho	writing: *graphology*
gymno	naked, bare, exposed: *gymnoplast*
gyneco	woman: *gynecology*
hagio	holy: *hagiography*
halo	salt: *halophyte*
hecto	hundred: *hectogram*
hedron	side, face: *tetrahedron*
helio	sun: *heliocentric*
hemi	half: *hemisphere*
hemo	blood: *hemoglobin*
hepato	liver: *hepatotoxin*
hepta	seven: *heptagon*
hetero	different: *heterosexual*
hexa	six: *hexagram*
histo	tissue: *histology*
holo	whole, complete: *holograph*
homeo	similar, like: *homeopathic*
homo	same: *homosexual*
hydro	water: *hydroplane*
hyeto	rain: *hyetology*
hygro	wet: *hygrometer*
hylo	matter: *hylotheism*
hymeno	membrane: *hymenotomy*
hyper	excessive, above, over: *hyperactive*
hypno	sleep: *hypnotism*
hypo	less than normal, insufficient, under: *hypodermic*
hypso	high: *hypsometer*
hyster	womb: *hysterectomy*
iatrics, iatry	medical treatment: *geriatrics; psychiatry*
itis	inflammation: *bronchitis*
ichthyo	fish: *ichthyology*
igni	fire: *ignite*
im	var. of in: *impolite*
in	not: *inappropriate*
inter	between, among: *intercept; interest; intercom*
intra	within: *intramural; intracranial*
intro	interior: *introspection*
iso	equal: *isometric*

juxta	close, near, beside: *juxtaposition*
kinesi	movement: *hyperkinesia*
labio	lip: *labiodental*
lacto	milk: *lactoprotein*
lepto	slender: *leptophyllous*
leuko	white: *leukocyte*
ligni	wood: *ligniform*
litho	stone: *lithograph*
logo	word, oral: *logotype*
luni	moon: *lunitidal*
macro	large: *macrocosm*
magni	great: *magnify*
mal	bad, evil: *malfunction; malcontent*
megalo	great: *megalopolis*
melano	black: *melanoderm*
mero	part: *meropia*
meso	middle: *mesomorphic*
meta	changed: *metamorphosis*
meter	measure: *diameter*
metro	measure: *metronome*
micro	small: *microscope*
milli	thousand: *millimeter*
miso	hatred: *misogyny*
mono	one, single: *monocable*
morpho	shape: *morphology*
multi	many: *multilateral*
myelo	spinal cord: *myeloma*
myo	muscle: *myocardiogram*
naso	nose: *nasology*
necro	dead body: *necrophilia*
neo	new: *neonatal*
nepho	cloud: *nephometer*
nephro	kidney: *nephrosis*
neuro	nerve: *neurobiology*
nocti	night: *noctilucen*
nomy	distribution, arrangement, management: *astronomy; economy*
non	not: *nonconformist*

noso	sickness: *nosology*
octa	eight: *octagon*
oculo	eye: *oculomotor*
odont	tooth: *orthodontics*
ology	a science or branch of knowledge: *biology; geology; psychology*
omni	all: *omnipresent*
oneiro	dream: *oneiromancy*
onto	being: *ontogeny*
oo	egg: *oocyte*
ophio	snake: *ophiology*
opthalm	eye: *ophthalmology*
ornitho	bird: *ornithology*
oro	mouth: *oropharynx*
ortho	straight: *orthodontia*
osteo	bone: *osteoporoses*
oto	ear: *otology*
ovi	egg: *ovicide*
oxy	sharp, keen, acid: *oxygen; oxymoron*
paleo	ancient, old: *paleobotany*
pan	all: *panacea*
para	close, beside: *parallel; paradox; parapsychology*
patho	disease: *pathology*
ped	foot: *pedestrian; pedal*
pedo	child: *pedology*
penta	five: *pentagram*
per	through, very: *pervert; pervade; perfect*
peri	around, very: *perimeter; periscope*
petro	stone: *petroglyph*
phago	eating: *phagocyte*
phile, philo	love: *pedophile; philogynist*
phlebo	vein: *phlebotomy*
phono	sound: *phonograph*
photo	light: *photochemical*
phreno	brain: *phrenology*
phyco	seaweed: *phycology*
phyllo	leaf: *phyllopod*
phylo	race, tribe, kind: *phylogeny*

physio	natural order, origin, form: *physiotherapy*
phyto	plant: *phytogenesis*
pisci	fish: *pisciform*
plano	flat: *planography*
pleuro	side (of body): *pleuropneumonia*
pluto	riches: *plutocracy*
pluvio	rain: *pluviometer*
pneumato	breath, spirit: *pneumatology*
pneumo	lung: *pneumonia*
pod	foot: *podiatry; cephalopod*
poly	many: *polyandrous; polyculture; polyethylene*
post	after: *postgraduate*
potent	powerful: *potentate; impotent*
pre	before: *predestination*
preter	beyond: *preternatural*
pro	for, forward, outward: *prologue; proceed; protract*
proto	first: *prototype*
pseudo	false: *pseudonym*
psycho	mind, spirit, soul: *psychology*
psychro	cold: *psychrometer*
ptero	wing, feather: *pterodactyl*
pulmo	lung: *pulmonary*
pyo	pus: *pyogenesis*
pyro	fire: *pyromaniac*
quadri	four: *quadriplegic*
quinque	five: *quinquevalent*
re	again: *remodel*
recti	straight: *rectify*
reni	kidney: *reniform*
retro	backward: *retroactive*
rheo	flow, current, stream: *rheoscope*
rhino	nose: *rhinology; rhinoceros*
rhizo	root: *rhizophagous*
sacchar	sugar: *saccharoid; saccharine*
sacro	sacred: *sacrosanct*
sangui	bloody, blood-red: *sanguine*
sapro	rotten: *saprogenic*
scato	excrement: *scatological*

schizo	split: *schizophrenic*
scient	knowledge: *omniscient; prescient*
sclero	hard: *scleroderma*
se	apart: *seduce; select*
seba	fatty: *sebaceous*
seleno	moon: *selenography*
semi	half, partially: *semicircle; semiautomatic*
sidero	iron, star: *siderostat*
somato	body: *somatological*
somna, somni	sleep: *somnambulant; insomnia*
sophy	science of: *philosophy; theosophy; anthroposophy*
speleo	cave: *speleology*
spermato	seed: *spermatozoan*
sphygmo	pulse: *sphygmometer*
spiro	breath: *spirograph*; coil: *spirochete*
splanchno	viscera: *splanchnopleure*
stat	position, stabilize: *thermostat; rheostat*
stauro	cross: *staurolite*
stelli	star: *stelliform*
steno	short: *stenographer*
stereo	solid: *stereogram; stereoscope*
stomato	mouth: *stomatoplasty*
stylo	column, tube, pillar: *stylolite*
sub	under, below, beneath: *subject; subvert; subordinate; subcommittee*
super	above, beyond: *superimpose; supersede; supernatural*
supra	above, over, beyond the limits of: *supramolecular; supra-orbital*
syn	with, together: *synthesis; synoptic; synonymous*
tachy	rapid: *tachycardia*
tauto	same: *tautological; tautonymous*
tele	distant: *telegraph; telecommunications*
thalasso	sea: *thalassocracy*
thanato	death: *thanatophobia; thanatopsis*
theo	god: *theocracy; theocentric*
thermo	heat, hot: *thermometer; thermos*
thio	sulfur: *thioaldehyde*

topo	place, local: *topography; topology*
toxico	poison: *toxicology*
trachy	rough: *trachycarpous*
trans	through, across, beyond: *transportation; transaction*
tri	three: *tricycle*
ultra	on the far side of, beyond: *ultraviolet; ultrasound*
un	not: *unreliable*
uni	one, single: *unicycle; unique; unit*
vari	different, miscellany: *variable; variation*
vene	to come: *intervene; contravene*
vorous	eating: *carnivorous*
xeno	foreign: *xenophobia*
zoo	living being, animal: *zoometry; zoological*
zygo	double: *zygodactyl*; yoke, yoke-shaped: *zygomorphic*

Chapter Four

Frequently Misused Words

"When I use a word," Humpty Dumpty said in a rather scornful tone, "it means just what I choose it to mean—nothing more nor less."

—LEWIS CARROLL, *THROUGH THE LOOKING-GLASS*

IN THIS LIST YOU WILL FIND words that are pronounced exactly alike but are different in spelling and meaning, such as *air* and *heir*, *beat* and *beet*, *cereal* and *serial*. Some of the words have similar, but not exactly the same pronunciation, such as *accept* and *except*, *prescribe* and *proscribe*. There are also words that don't sound alike and are not directly related, but are confused because of their association with each other, such as *imply* and *infer*, *complex* and *compound*.

The word groups are listed according to the word that comes first in the alphabet. For example, both *access* and *excess* appear under the heading for words that begin with "A." The word *excess* is not listed again under "E." However, all of the words on the misused words list are also listed in the index in alphabetical order, indicating the page on which you will find them.

A

abbé   a member of the French secular clergy; a title of respect for any ecclesiastic

abbey   a monastery under the supervision of an abbott or a convent under the supervision of an abbess

abbreviate   to shorten by contraction or omission, such as *agcy., corp., Gov., Dr., Rev.*

abridge   to reduce or condense, such as a summary of a report or article: *abridge a book*; to lessen the duration or scope of; to curtail: *abridge a person's freedom*

abdicate   renounce or relinquish, such as a right: *He will abdicate the throne to marry a commoner.*; resign, quit; abandon; repudiate

abrogate   to abolish or annul by formal means; to repeal; put aside; cancel; revoke; rescind; nullify: *to abrogate a law*

arrogate   to claim presumptuously; to assume without right: *arrogate the right to make decisions*; to attribute or assign to another; ascribe

abdominal   of, in, or for the abdomen: *exercise to strengthen the abdominal wall*

abominable   repugnantly hateful; loathsome: *an abominable crime*; very bad, poor, or inferior: *abominable taste in clothes*

ability   a general word for power, native or acquired, enabling one to do things well: *an ability for math*

capacity   actual or potential ability to perform or withstand: *a capacity for hard work*

faculty   a natural ability for a particular kind of action: *a faculty for choosing the right friends*

talent   native ability or aptitude in a special field: *a talent for art or music*

abject   debasing, degrading; contemptible; despicable: *an abject liar*;
  miserable; wretched: *abject poverty*

object   a thing or person to which an action is directed: *an object of
  affection*; target; destination; intention; motive

abjure   repudiate, recant, or retract; to renounce under oath, forswear:
  abjure allegiance; *abjure a confession*

adjure   to charge or command earnestly, often under the threat of a
  penalty; to entreat solemnly: *to adjure the witness to tell the truth*

abscission   an act of cutting off; the process by which plant parts, such as
  leaves, are shed

incision   a surgical cut into soft tissue; a notch as in the edge of a leaf

absence   the state of being away; the time during which one is away; lack:
  absence of evidence

absents   to keep (oneself) away: *She absents herself from all meetings.*

absorb   assimilate; consume; soak up: *A sponge absorbs water.*

adsorb   gather a substance on a surface: *Charcoal will adsorb gasses.*

abstruse   hard to understand; esoteric: *abstruse theories*; recondite,
  incomprehensible, unfathomable, arcane

obtuse   not quick or alert in perception, feeling, or intellect; dull, blunt,
  unfeeling, tactless, insensitive: *an obtuse statement made without considering
  its effect*; slow, dim; boorish; indistinctly felt or perceived, as pain or
  sound

abuse   mishandle; misapply; pervert; revile, malign;
  mistreat: *The greater the power, the more dangerous the abuse.*

disabuse   to free a person from deception, error, or misconception: *I want
  to disabuse you of your opinion of the gentleman.*

abysmal   immeasurably deep or extreme, fathomless: *an abysmal misunderstanding*

abyssal   relating to the great depths of the oceans

accede   assent or yield; give consent; agree: *accede to the terms of the agreement*; to attain an office; succeed: *accede to the throne*

concede   yielding without necessarily agreeing: *He conceded the election before all the votes were in.*

exceed   to go beyond the bounds: *exceed the speed limit*; outdo; beat

accelerate   hasten the occurrence of: *accelerate reforms*; to move or go faster; to progress faster: *accelerate educational programs*

exhilarate   to invigorate, animate, elate, stimulate: *A brisk walk will exhilarate you.*

accept   receive: *She will accept the award.*; answer affirmatively: *I accept your invitation.*

except   leave out; exclude: *present company excepted*; with the exclusion of: *Everyone was there except for the guest of honor.*

access   permission to use, speak with, or enter; a way to approach: *Access to the stage is through the back door.*

excess   an extreme amount or degree: *an excess of food and drink*; superabundance; immoderate indulgence: *A hundred pairs of shoes is an excess.*

accessible   easy to approach, reach, enter, or use: *an accessible road*; attainable: *accessible evidence*

assessable   able to determine the value of; something that is subject to a tax or fine: *an assessable piece of property*

acclamation   enthusiastic approval: *The performance was met with acclamation.*

acclimation   adaptation of an organism to its climatic environment: *acclimation to the cold*

accrue   accumulate, grow, increase; added as a matter of periodic gain: *accrue interest on a savings account*

ecru   a pale beige color, as unbleached linen

acentric   having no center; not centered

eccentric   strange, weird, bizarre; deviating from customs or practice; erratic; peculiar: *an eccentric hermit*

acetic   of, relating to, or containing acetic acid or vinegar: *The wine had become acetic.*

aesthetic   relating to a sense of the beautiful; artistic: *The decorator has a real sense of the aesthetic.*; discriminating, cultivated, refined; concerned with pure emotion and sensation as opposed to pure intellectuality: *an aesthetic actress*

ascetic   one who leads an austere life: *an ascetic nun*

acidulous   moderately acid or tart; sharp; caustic: *an acidulous critique*

assiduous   constant; persevering; unremitting: *assiduous investigation*; continuous; tireless; diligent: *an assiduous pursuit of perfection*

actually   an actual or existing fact; really; genuinely, without exaggeration: *The deceased was actually frightened to death.*

literally   in a literal manner; word for word: *literally translated*; actually; without exaggeration or inaccuracy: *The platoon was literally wiped out in the explosion.*

virtually   for the most part; almost completely; just about: *He was virtually scared out of his wits.*

[*Literally*, like *virtually*, is widely used as an intensifier meaning "in effect," which contradicts the earlier meaning of "actually, without exaggeration." *Virtually* is often used to mean "actually" when its definition is "for practical purposes though not in name."]

action   the process of being active; energetic activity; effect or influence: *a man of action*

auction   a publicly held sale at which goods are sold to the highest bidder: *I made the highest bid at the auction.*

aesthetician   a person trained to administer facials and give advice on makeup and care of the skin
anesthetist   a person who administers anesthetics: *I spoke with the anesthetist before my surgery.*

ad   advertisement, advertising: *an ad agency*
add   to make an addition; to say or write further; to include: *Be sure to add the tax.*

adage   traditional saying; proverb: *An old adage states that you reap what you sow.*
axiom   self-evident truth; universally accepted principle or rule: *"As sure as day follows night" is an axiom.*

adapt   fit, adjust, alter, or modify: *She will adapt the costume to fit.*
adept   thoroughly proficient; an expert: *He is adept at landscaping difficult lots.*
adopt   take another's child as one's own: *I will adopt my late sister's boy.*; to accept: *adopt a proposal*

addenda   something added: *Please check the addenda to the agenda.*
agenda   list of things to do; items to cover in a meeting: *All of the proposals are on the agenda.*

addict   one who is physiologically or psychologically dependent on a substance such as alcohol or a narcotic; one who is addicted to an activity or habit; a fanatic
edict   a decree; an authoritative proclamation or command; a dictum, pronouncement

addition   the act of adding or uniting: *We are going to have an addition to our family.*

edition   one of a series of printings; a version of anything, printed or not: *This is the latest edition of the Word program.*

adherence   steady devotion, support, or allegiance: *rigid adherence to the law*

adherents   a disciple or devotee; those who follow or uphold a leader or cause; bound by contract: *adherents to the Geneva Convention*

adieu   good-bye; farewell; the act of leaving: *He bade his friends adieu.*

ado   bustle, fuss; flurry; confusion; turmoil; commotion: *much ado about nothing*

adjoin   close to or in contact with: *The island nearly adjoins the mainland.*; attach; affix

adjourn   postpone; suspend a meeting to a future time: *adjourn the court*; to go to another place: *They will adjourn to the bar after the last seminar.*

adjunct   appendix, supplement; an aide, attaché, or assistant: *an adjunct to the consul*

admission   access: *Admission is on the side of the building.*; entrance fee: *For the price of admission, you get to see two shows*; confession of guilt: *His admission of the crime got him a lighter sentence.*

admittance   the act of entering; the permission to enter: *Only members are allowed admittance.*

adolescence   the period between puberty and adulthood, usually considered the teen years

adolescents   youths, teenagers, minors

adversary   a person, group, or force that opposes or attacks; opponent; enemy; foe; one who is an opponent in a contest; a contestant; one who fights determinedly and relentlessly: *He was a worthy adversary.*

adversity   catastrophe, disaster; trouble, misery; adverse fortune or fate; a condition marked by misfortune: *In times of adversity, she crumbles.*

antagonist   a person who opposes another, often in a hostile manner: *The man was his antagonist in a duel.*; an enemy, foe; the adversary of the hero or protagonist in a literary work

adverse   antagonistic: *adverse criticism*; unlucky; disastrous; unfavorable; catastrophic: *an extremely adverse reaction to a medication*; an opposing position; opposite: *the adverse page.*

averse   unwilling; loath; a feeling of antipathy, repugnance or great distaste: *He was averse to overcrowded places.*

[*Adverse* is seldom used of people. It pertains more often to effects or events: *adverse reviews; adverse conditions; adverse trends. Averse* is used of people and means opposed or disinclined: *We are not averse to staying in town another day. Averse* is usually followed by *to.*]

advert   to comment; to refer to: *He adverted to the news release.*; to turn attention to: *The chairman adverted to the agenda.*

avert   to turn away or aside: *avert one's eyes*; ward off: *to avert evil*; prevent: *avert an accident*

divert   to turn from a path or course; deflect; to veer: *divert one's talents to trivial pursuits*

advice   an opinion or recommendation offered as a guide to conduct; an admonition; a warning: *Timely advice kept them from making a mistake.*

advise   to give counsel to; to offer a suggestion, caution: *I advise you not to drive so fast on this road.*; notify, apprise: *She advised me of the job opportunity.*

aegis   protection; support; sponsorship; auspices: *The fundraising event was under the aegis of the Literary Arts Society.*

ages   epochs, eras, periods: *Human nature has not changed a great deal throughout the ages.*

aerie   the nest of a bird of prey, a house or fortress located high on a hill or mountain

airy   breezy; jaunty; sprightly; lively: *airy songs*; unsubstantial; unreal; imaginary; fanciful; lofty

affect   to pretend; influence: *It will affect the outcome.*
effect   a result; an influence: *His protest had no effect.*

[The words *affect* and *effect* are among the most frequently confused words. *Affect* means to bring about a change, to move emotionally, or to infect, as a disease. Its core meaning is *to evoke a usually strong mental or emotional response from*. *Effect* means *consequence, outcome, upshot*. Its core meaning is *something brought about by a cause*.]

affective   caused by or expressing feelings; emotional; causing emotion or feeling: *It was an affective scene that brought tears to the audience.*
effective   producing the intended result: *Her effective speech caused many to volunteer.*; actually in force: *The new law becomes effective on January 1.*

affluent   wealthy: *The countess was quite affluent.*; abundant; flowing freely
effluent   to flow out; an outflow of waste: *The effluent from the broken sewer pipe was foul smelling.*

afterward   at a later or subsequent time: *We attended the meeting and afterward we went to dinner.*
afterword   a concluding section, commentary, etc. as of a book: *The author's widow wrote the afterword.*

aggravate   to make worse: *The smoky room aggravated her asthma.*; to annoy: *Don't aggravate the substitute teacher.*
irritate   exasperate; provoke; inflame or chafe: *Her incessant chatter irritates me.*

aggression   an unprovoked offensive, attack, or invasion; an encroachment: *an aggression upon civil rights*; overt or suppressed hostility
egression   egress; a going out

aid   to help or assist: *I hope you will aid me with the project.*
aide   an assistant: *I have so much work that I need an aide.*

ail   to feel ill; to make uneasy: *What ails him?*
ale   a fermented alcoholic beverage: *Order me a mug of ale.*

air   the atmosphere: *The air is fresher in the mountains.*; expose: *air griev-
ances*; a tune: *She hummed an air.*
err   be mistaken or incorrect; to go astray morally; sin; transgress: *To err is
human.*
heir   one who inherits an
estate: *Her nephew is her only heir.*

aisle   passageway: *The bride's father escorted her down the aisle.*
I'll   contraction of *I will.*
isle   small island: *The isle is only a short distance from shore.*

albumen   the white of an egg
albumin   a class of simple, sulfur-containing, water-soluble proteins

align   to bring into a line or alignment; straighten; to join with others in a
cause: *They align themselves with the environmental movement.*
A-line   a style of dress or other garment consisting of A-shaped panels that
give increasing fullness toward the hemline: *an A-line skirt*

alimentary   relating to food or nutrition: *alimentary canal*
elementary   pertaining to elements, or first principles: *elementary grammar*;
simple, easy facts: *It's elementary,   Dr. Watson.*

all   the total entity of: *All of us are going.*; whole number or amount: *giving
it all away*
awl   a pointed tool for boring holes: *The carpenter used an awl to make a hole
for the doorknob.*

allay   soften, assuage: lay to rest or lull into a sense of security: *She tried to allay her child's fears.*

alley   a passage, a narrow back street: *Our garage is off the back alley.*

alloy   a lower-quality metal mixed with a more valuable one; to debase, impair, or adulterate; fusion, blend, composite: *Coins are often alloys.*

ally   unify, join; a partner, friend, or confederate: *Canada was our ally in World War II.*

allege   to assert without proof; to state; attest: *They allege that he stole the jewelry.*

aver   to express an opinion, judgment, or position: *They aver that he is the type who would steal anything.* In legal use, *aver* means to "allege as fact."

allergen   any substance that induces an allergy, such as pollen, grasses, certain foods, and medications

allergic   pertaining to an allergy: *allergic to peanuts*

allergy   an abnormal reaction of the body to an allergen, manifested by runny nose, skin rash, wheezing, etc.; hypersensitivity to the reintroduction of an allergen

alliterate   to use two or more words having the same initial sound, as in: *Sister Suzie sews shirts for sixty-six seasick sailors.*

illiterate   unable to read and write; having little or no formal education: *He has a lot of native intelligence but he is illiterate.*

all mighty   all strong, powerful, enormous, etc.: *The fighters were all mighty men.*

almighty   omnipotent, as God; supreme, sovereign

all over   finished: *It is all over now.*; everywhere: *There were people all over the place.*

allover   extending over the entire surface, as a decorative pattern: *an allover design of red roses*

allowed   permitted; given as one's share: *The host is allowed ten percent of the entrance fee.*

aloud   spoken in a normal tone and volume; vocally: *Read the story aloud.*

all ready   everyone is prepared, available, or willing: *We are all ready to go to dinner now.*

already   so soon; previously: *Oh, but I've already eaten.*

all right   satisfactory; safe and sound: *I'm feeling all right now.*; expressing consent or assent: *It is all right to leave the table.*

all-right   acceptable: *He's an all-right kind of guy.*

alright   nonstandard for *all right*; often used in informal writing: *I'm alright, thank you.*

all together   in a group: *They were all together at the engagement party.*

altogether   wholly, completely: *It is altogether acceptable to come without a gift.*

allude   hint, intimate, suggest; to refer to casually; an indirect reference: *allude to a mutual friend*

elude   shun, dodge, escape, avoid, evade: *elude the police*

allusive   having reference to something implied or referred: *The clever remark was allusive to Shakespeare's* Taming of the Shrew.

elusive   hard to express or define: *an elusive concept*; tricky, slippery; baffling; shifty: *an elusive felon*

illusive   deceptive; misleading: *an illusive alibi*; false; unreal; imaginary: *an illusive reference to ghosts and goblins*

alluvion   overflow; flood

alluvium   a deposit of sand, mud, silt, or gravel formed by flowing

eluvium   a deposit of soil, dust, or rock debris formed by the decomposition of rock

illuvium   the material accumulated through soil that has been leached out of another layer of soil

all ways   every manner possible: *In all ways he is kind and just.*

always   at all times: *She is always late.*

a lot   many, a large number: *There are a lot of pencils in the package.*

allot   distribute or parcel out; set apart: *Allot no more than thirty percent of your income for rent.*

aloud   with the normal tone of a speaking voice; vocally: *He read aloud in class.*

allowed   permitted: *The children were allowed to leave early.*; admitted; acknowledged; conceded: *He allowed that he had made a mistake.*

altar   a table or platform used in a church service or ceremonial rite: *They knelt at the altar for communion.*

alter   change: *alter a will*; adjust: *She'll need to alter her wedding gown to make it fit.*

altitude   elevation; extent or distance upward; height: *The altitude of the Washington Monument is 555 feet.*

attitude   position; disposition; feeling regarding a person or thing: *a negative attitude*; posture that is expressive of an emotion: *an attitude of indifference*

amend   to alter, modify, rephrase; to add or subtract from: *Congress may amend the tax bill.*

amends   reparation or compensation for a loss, damage, or injury of any kind; recompense; to make amends: *He tried to make amends for his rudeness by bringing flowers.*

emend   to edit or change (a text) to remove errors; to correct: *We must emend the text before the book goes to print.*

amiable   friendly and pleasant in temperament: *She is an amiable hostess.*

amicable   characterized by showing goodwill; peaceable: *They reached an amicable settlement.*

among   in association or connection with; surrounded by: *You are among friends.*

between   in the space separating two objects: *It was hard to choose between vanilla and chocolate.*

[*Among* is used when more than two persons or things are involved. *Between* is used when only two persons or things are involved.]

amour   a secret love affair

armoire   a wardrobe or cupboard with doors and shelves

armor   a protective covering; anything that serves as protection

amoral   neither moral nor immoral; unaware of or indifferent to questions of right or wrong: *Sometimes lawbreakers are simply amoral.*

immoral   violating moral principles; bad; wicked: *Stealing is an immoral act.*

amputation   cutting off, especially of a body part: *After the amputation of his leg he was fitted for a prosthesis.*

imputation   an accusation; an attribution, as of fault: *His imputation was completely off base.*

analgesic   a remedy that relieves or allays pain: *The doctor prescribed an analgesic for her aching muscles.*

anesthetic   an agent that produces insensibility: *He was still groggy from the anesthetic.*

antiseptic   an agent that destroys bacteria: *She used an antiseptic ointment on the cut.*

analyst   one who analyzes: *He's a CIA analyst.*

annalist   a writer of historical records: *He writes annals of war.*

anarchy   the absence of laws or government: *The fall of the empire was followed by chaos and anarchy.*

aristocracy   rule by elite or privileged upper class: *The governing body was composed of the country's most powerful aristocracy.*

democracy   government by the people: *The United States is a democracy.*
oligarchy   government by the few: *The citizens have no voice in an oligarchy.*
plutocracy   government in which the wealthy class rules: *In a plutocracy, there is little regard for the poor.*

androgenous   tending to produce male offspring; capable of developing certain male sexual characteristics
androgynous   being both male and female; hermaphroditic; having an ambiguous sexual identity

anecdote   a brief story relating an interesting or amusing event: *His anecdote was very funny.*
antidote   a remedy for counteracting a poison or disease: *She was given an antidote immediately.*

angel   a heavenly creature: *Your mother is such an angel.*
angle   a geometric figure; an angular projection; a projecting corner: *the angles of a building*; a viewpoint; standpoint: *He looked at the situation from every angle.*

annals   a record of events; chronicles, history
annuals   books or reports that are published annually
annuls   makes null or void; abolishes; cancels; invalidates; rescinds

ant   an insect: *No one invited an ant to this picnic.*
aunt   a female relative: *I invited my aunt to the wedding.*

antecedence   the act of going before; precedence
antecedents   ancestors; forerunners; the history, events, and characteristics of one's earlier life

anterior   located in front; situated before or at the front of; fore (opposed to *posterior*); going before in time or sequence; preceding; earlier: *events anterior to the outbreak of war*

exterior   external, outer; originating or acting from the outside; being on the outer side: *the exterior surface*; suitable for outdoor use: *exterior paint*; outward form or appearance: *She has a calm exterior, but inside she is frightened.*

interior   located inside: *The interior of the building is well lit.*; inner: *She looks fragile but she has an inner strength.*

antic   a prank; playful trick; caper; ludicrous, funny

antique   belonging to the past; bygone; archaic

anxious   worried, troubled; full of mental distress or uneasiness: *She felt anxious about her child's high fever.*; excited: *I'm anxious about the game.*

eager   earnestly desirous, enthusiastic: *She was eager to see him again.*

[These words once had different meanings but *anxious* is now an acceptable synonym for *eager* in some cases: *He was anxious to see the play.*]

any body   any group: *Any body of protestors can become difficult to control.*; any physical body: *Although we searched the area where the murder occurred, we couldn't find any body.*

anybody   any person: *You may choose anybody you wish to go with you.*

any more   any amount: *We don't have any more candy.*

anymore   any longer; presently: *I don't make candy anymore.*

any one   any single member of a group: *Any one of you might be affected by the changes.*

anyone   any person at all: *Has anyone seen my book?*

any way   in any manner: *You may wear the scarf any way you wish.*

anyway   in any case; anyhow; nonetheless: *She knew it was wrong but she did it anyway.*

aphagia   difficulty or pain in swallowing

aphasia   inability to speak or understand spoken or written language, due to disease or injury of the brain

apiary   a place in which a colony of bees is kept
aviary   a large cage or house for birds

apologies   written or spoken expressions of regret: *She will make apologies for her rudeness.*; excuses or justifications, as for a cause or doctrine; vindications
apologize   to offer an apology or excuse for some fault, insult, failure, or injury: *You should apologize for being so insensitive.*

appellant   a person who appeals a court decision
appellate   the power to review and decide appeals, as a court

apposition   placing together or bringing into proximity; juxtaposition; the addition of one thing to another thing: *The new parking structure was built in apposition to the library.* In grammar, a syntactic relation between expressions having the same function and relation to other elements in the sentence, with the second expression identifying the first: *John, my old boyfriend, showed up at my wedding.* The phrase, *my old boyfriend*, is in apposition with *John*.
opposition   resistance; antagonism or hostility; those opposing or protesting something or someone: *The opposition is getting more votes.*

a portion   any part of any whole; segment, section: *I read only a portion of the book.*
apportion   to distribute or allocate proportionally; divide or assign: *Apportion the bonus among the staff.*

appraise   assess; determine the worth of: *She asked the jeweler to appraise her diamond ring.*
apprise   give notice of; acquaint; inform: *He will apprise the client of the fee.*

approbate   to approve officially: *approbate a legal matter*

reprobate   depraved, unprincipled, or wicked person: *a drug-dealing reprobate*

arbiter   a person empowered to judge or make determinations: *She will act as arbiter in the dispute.*

orbiter   a space probe designed to orbit a planetary body: *The orbiter will land shortly.*

arc   a curved line; something shaped like a bow or arch: *the arc of a rainbow*

ark   a place of refuge; a large, commodious boat

area   surface, extent, or range: *He combed the area for evidence.*

aria   a melody; a solo as in an opera: *Her aria was beautifully sung.*

arraign   call before a court to answer to an indictment; to accuse or charge: *They will arraign the suspect in the morning.*

arrange   place in a certain order; adjust properly; array, group, sort, classify: *Arrange the cards in alphabetical order.*

arrant   downright, thorough, unmitigated, notorious, utter, confirmed, flagrant: *an arrant playboy*

errant   deviating from the proper course; straying; moving aimlessly: *an errant breeze*

arrhythmic   a disturbance in rhythm, as in the heartbeat

eurhythmic   characterized by a pleasing rhythm; harmoniously proportioned

arsine   a colorless, flammable gas used in chemical warfare

arson   malicious burning of property

artistic   exhibiting taste; conforming to standards of art; involving aesthetics

autistic   a developmental disorder characterized by emotional detachment and difficulty in communicating with others

ascent   the act or process of moving upward: *The plane made a rapid ascent.*

assent   to express agreement as to a plan; concur; consent: *She nodded her assent.*

aspire   have a strong hope or ambition; to strive toward an end: *They aspire to greatness.*

inspire   fill with high emotion; to guide by divine influence; stimulate creativity: *Her beauty could inspire a work of art.*

assay   an analysis of a substance, esp. of an ore or drug: *His find required an assay to determine its value.*

essay   try; subject to a test; a short literary composition: *She wrote an essay for her final exam.*

asses   more than one donkey or dolt

assess   to appraise or evaluate; estimate value for tax purposes

assistance   help; aid; support: *Can I be of some assistance?*

assistants   people who give help and support; aides: *My assistants will help you with that.*

astrict   to bind fast; constrain: *The court will astrict the witness from making a public statement at this time.*

constrict   cause to contract or shrink; to draw in; compress; to slow the natural course of: *Too many rules can constrict a child's development.*

assume   to take for granted: *Don't assume the old bridge is safe.*; suppose; postulate; to take upon oneself: *assume an obligation*; to take on, adopt: *assume a virtue*; to feign: *assume an innocent demeanor*; to take on the debts or obligations of another: *assume the loan*

presume   belief on reasonable grounds; in law, to assume as true in the absence of proof to the contrary; to undertake with unwarrantable boldness; to undertake without permission: *presume to speak for someone else;* go too far in taking liberties; also some of the same meanings as *assume,* such as *presuppose* and *take for granted*

attendance   the act of attending; the number of persons present: *The attendance was larger than ever before.*
attendants   persons who are present, as an event or meeting: *the attendants were mainly members of the club*; escorts; companions; servants

aural   pertaining to an aura; pertaining to the ear or the sense of hearing
oral   spoken: *an oral history; an oral exam*; pertaining to the mouth: *the oral cavity*

auricle   outer portion of the ear; a part resembling an ear
oracle   one who is wise, authoritative, or highly regarded; a divine revelation

auteur   a film director or producer who controls a production and gives the film its unique style
hauteur   arrogance; a haughty manner

automation   a mechanical device that functions automatically; the process of automating
automaton   a mechanical figure that acts as if by its own power; robot; one who acts in a routine manner without apparent active intelligence

avenge   to exact satisfaction for; vindicate: *He will avenge his partner's death.*
revenge   to exact punishment for a wrong in a resentful spirit: *She was determined to get revenge for the insulting remark.*

[*Avenge* and *revenge* were formerly interchangeable, but now they convey diverse ideas. *Avenge* means inflicting punishment as an act of retributive justice: *to avenge a murder by bringing the criminal to trial. Revenge* is now defined as inflicting pain to retaliate for real or fancied wrongs: *He will revenge himself upon the man who libeled him.*]

avocation   a hobby in addition to a principal occupation: *The judge's avocation is acting in little theater productions.*; a person's regular occupation or calling

evocation   a calling forth: *an evocation of earlier times*

avoid   elude; keep away from; shun

ovoid   egg-shaped

avulsion   a tearing away; a part torn off: *The storm's runoff caused an avulsion of the stream's bank.*

evulsion   plucking or pulling out; forcible extraction: *The evulsion of her baby tooth was painless.*

revulsion   disgust, repulsion, aversion; a strong feeling of repugnance: *His filthy language fills me with revulsion.*

auger   a tool used to bore holes, as in ice or wood; a large tool for boring into the earth

augur   a prophet; soothsayer; to prophesy; to be a sign: *The heavy rain augurs a bountiful harvest.*

aught   anything whatever; any part: *for aught I know*; a cipher; zero

naught   nothing; be without result: *come to naught*; lost; ruined

ought   should; duty or obligation: *You ought to go to the memorial service.*

avoid   elude, escape; shun; prevent from happening: *Avoid a possible accident by crossing only on the green light.*

evade   dodge, fence, prevaricate; to escape from or get around by trickery: *She tried to evade the rules.*

[*Evade* usually has a negative connotation. It means to elude by craft or slyness. *Avoid* means to succeed in keeping away from a dangerous or undesirable experience. In law, to *avoid* means to make void or of no effect; to invalidate. *Tax avoidance*, for example, could be legitimate, while *tax evasion* implies nonpayment of taxes, as through the failure to report taxable income.]

a way   a manner: *He showed me a way to fix the problem.*

away   from here or there: *go away*; aside; in another direction: *turn away from the regular path*; out of one's possession: *give away your earthly goods*

aweigh   (of an anchor) hanging just clear of the bottom: *Anchors aweigh, my boys. Anchors aweigh!*

a while   a period of time: *He had to wait a while for the bus. It has been a while since they've seen each other.*

awhile   for a short time; for an interval of time: *Please stay awhile.*

axil   angle between a branch and stem

axle   supporting shaft on which a wheel revolves

B

---

back up   to support someone's opinion or order: *I back up his no-smoking rule.*; to move backward: *Back up and give him some air!*

backup   one who supports or reinforces another: *I'm his backup*; (computers) a copy or duplicate version of a file, program, or computer system: *I made a backup of the file.*

bad   not good: *bad luck*; wicked; defective: *a bad part*; unsound; false; disobedient: *Bad dog!*

bade   past tense of bid: *She bade him goodbye for the last time.*

bail   money to release a prisoner: *I had to bail him out of jail.*; remove water, as from a boat: *They had to bail very fast to keep the boat from sinking.*

bale   a large, bound package, as a bale of hay: *Stack the bales in the barn.*

bailer   a bucket, dipper, or other container used for bailing

bailor   a person who delivers personal property in bailment

baited   lured, enticed: *She baited him with a seductive dance.*; placed bait on a hook

bated   lessened the force of; with breath drawn in or held: *She spoke with bated breath.*

bald   bare; without hair: *When he grew older, he became bald.*

balled   wound into a ball: *She balled the yarn.*

bawled   shouted; sobbed loudly: *The baby bawled when his lollipop was taken away.*

baleful   malignant in intent; sinister; ominous; injurious; pernicious: *His baleful actions were terrifying.*

baneful   causing death or destruction: *a baneful invasion*; poisonous: *baneful castor beans*

balky   pigheaded; contrary; stubborn; obstinate; perverse; mulish: *The balky child refused to put on her shoes.*

bulky   large and cumbersome; massive; ponderous; unwieldy: *The bulky package was hard to maneuver through the door.*

ball   a round body, as a baseball, tennis ball, etc.; a game played with a ball; a dance: *after the ball was over*

bawl   to cry or wail; a loud shout, outcry; scold: *Your mom will bawl you out for being late.*

ballet   a classical dance; a company of ballet dancers

ballot   a slip of paper on which a voter marks his or her choice; voting in general

balmy   mild and refreshing; soft; soothing; *a balmy breeze*; producing balm: *balmy plants*; crazy; foolish; eccentric: *a balmy old hermit*

barmy   containing or resembling barm, the yeast formed on malt liquors while fermenting; frothy: *a barmy drink*

balsa   a tropical American tree of the bombax family, yielding a very light wood used for rafts and toys: *The toy airplane was made of balsa wood.*

balsam   a fragrant resin exuded from certain trees; any of various plants belonging to the genus Impatiens; any agency that heals, soothes, or restores: *the balsam of kindness*

band   group of musicians: *a jazz band*; a gang: *a band of thieves*; a thin, flat strip of material for binding; a stripe used as decoration; a ring: *a wedding band*

banned   prohibited; forbidden, barred; outlawed: *Smoking is now banned in most restaurants.*

banded   secured with a band: *He banded the newspapers for recycling.*

bandied   passed back and forth; circulated freely: *News of her shocking behavior was bandied about all over the little town.*

banquet   lavish meal; feast; ceremonious dinner: *The awards were followed by a banquet.*

banquette   a long bench; embankment; a ledge on a buffet; platform: *Mary and Sheldon will be sitting on the banquette.*

bard   a poet; the bard: *William Shakespeare*

barred   provided with bars, as a prison; banned: *They barred the windows against intruders.*

bare   unadorned, plain: *Tell me the bare facts.*; naked; without covering or clothing: *bare midriff*; scarcely sufficient: *the bare necessities*

bear   to give birth to: *bear a child*; to suffer; endure; undergo: *bear the blame*; to bring: *bear gifts*; to render; afford; give: *bear witness, bear testimony*; an animal: *a polar bear*

barely   hardly; only just; almost not: *She barely made it to work on time.*; scantily: *She's barely clothed.*; sparsely
barley   a grain used as food and in making beer, ale, and whiskey

baring   uncovering; undressing; exposing: *He removed his shirt, baring his chest.*
bearing   a person's demeanor, including posture and gestures: *She has a regal bearing.*; bringing forth: *a tree bearing fruit*

baron   a member of nobility; a person of great power in a particular area: *an oil baron*
barren   unproductive; unfruitful; not producing results; infertile: *The queen was barren.*

barrenness   the state of being barren: *the barrenness of the land*
baroness   the wife of a baron; a woman holding a baronial title in her own right

barret   a small cap worn in the Middle Ages by soldiers and ecclesiastics
barrette   a clasp used to hold one's hair in place
beret   a soft cap with a close-fitting headband and a wide, round top

basal   at the base; forming a basis; fundamental; basic
basil   an aromatic herb used in cooking

base   the bottom support; that on which something stands; a fundamental principle; basis; foundation: *Place the vase on the base.*
bass   (pronounced bāss) in music, low in pitch or range, a bass voice or instrument: *He sings bass.*

bases   plural of base and of basis: *All the bases are covered.*
basis   the principal constituent; a basic fact, amount, standard, etc., used in reaching conclusions; groundwork: *This is the basis for our decision.*

basses   more than one person singing bass: *There were three basses in the choir*; more than one bass instrument: *The orchestra had two string basses.*

bath   water used for washing or soaking the body: *taking a bath*; a liquid in which something is dipped
bathe   to take or give a bath: *bathe the baby*; to go swimming: *bathe at the seashore*

bauble   a showy ornament; trinket, gewgaw
bobble   a repeated, jerky movement; a fumbling of a baseball; an error; mistake
bubble   a round body of gas contained in a liquid; a dome or domelike structure; a temporary change: *a real estate bubble*

bazaar   a shop; a fair where merchandise is sold: *I found some lovely vases at the bazaar.*
bizarre   strikingly unconventional or far-fetched: *He was behaving in a very bizarre way.*

be   exist, live; take place; happen; to belong; attend: *I'll be at the concert.*
bee   an insect, as a bumblebee or honeybee; a community social gathering: *a sewing bee; a spelling bee*

beach   the shore of a body of water: *We sunned ourselves on the beach.*
beech   tree with light colored bark and edible nuts: *We planted beech trees in the front yard.*

beat   strike repeatedly; vanquish; sound a signal: *beat a drum*; a rhythmical unit of time: *The metronome set the beat.*
beet   a vegetable with a (usually) dark red bulbous root: *My mother made pickled beets.*

beatify   to make blessedly happy; to exalt above all others: *They beatify their saints.*

beautify   to make or become beautiful: *They beautify themselves for the ball.*

beau   boyfriend of a girl or woman: *I think my sister has a beau.*
bow   something bent, curved, or arched; a knot usually having two ends and two loops: *She tied her sash into a bow.*

beaut   (informal) someone or something that is beautiful or amazing: *His girlfriend is a beaut.*
boot   protective footgear covering the foot and part of the leg: *Be sure to wear boots in the woods.*
butte   a hill that has sloping sides and a flat top: *He stood on the butte to survey the valley.*

beer   a fermented alcoholic beverage: *He went to the tavern for a beer.*
bier   a funeral litter: *They placed the coffin on the bier.*

bell   a hollow instrument that is rung by the strokes of a clapper, hammer, etc.: *She rang a bell to summon her servants.*
belle   the most popular woman among many: *She was the belle of the ball.*

bellow   a loud cry of an animal; to roar; to utter in a loud voice
bellows   a device producing a strong current of air; the lungs

below   under; in a lower place; beneath the surface of the water: *what lies below*
billow   a surge of the sea; a swell, breaker, crest; to swell out as by the wind: *The boat's sails billow in the wind.*

berg   iceberg
burg   city or town

berry   a fleshy, edible fruit: *She made a berry cobbler.*

bury   to conceal; to place in a grave: *They will bury her tomorrow.*

berth   a built-in bed or bunk: *Joey wants to sleep on the top berth.*; a docking space

birth   beginning of existence; origin: *the birth of the blues*

beseech   pray, petition, beg eagerly for; implore urgently: *I beseech you to forgive me.*

besiege   to crowd around; beset, pester, harass, hound: *The actor was besieged by adoring fans.*

beside   at the side of: *She stood beside me.*

besides   in addition to: *Who is going besides me?*

better   more useful, desirable or suitable: *This is a much better choice.*

bettor   one who makes a wager: *The bettor goes to Las Vegas as often as he can.*

Bi-Words

Some words with the prefix *bi-* have no standard usage and need to be qualified whenever they are used. For instance, if you called for a *biweekly* meeting, you'd have to explain whether you meant two times a week or every other week.

biweekly either twice a week or once every two weeks

bimonthly either twice a month or once every two months

biquarterly two times during each three-month period of the year

biannual occurring twice a year

biennial occurring every two years

biyearly either twice a year or once every two years

biennium a two-year period

bicentennial happening once every two hundred years

bimillenium a period of two thousand years; a two thousandth anniversary

bight part of a rope; bend in the shore; gulf
bite cut or wound with the teeth: *Does your dog bite?*
byte adjacent bits processed by a computer

billed charged: *I was billed for the repair*; listed: *She was billed just after the lead actor.*; advertised: *It was billed as a comedy.*
build to construct: *He will build the garage himself.*; develop or increase: *build up a bank account*

bland soothing; affable, mild amiable; not highly flavored; tasteless; unemotional: *a bland response*
blend mix inseparably together: *blend the sauce*; compound; mingle; combine; unite

blatant offensively noisy or loud; brazenly obvious: *a blatant show of wealth*
flagrant disgraceful; monstrous; obviously evil; shockingly evident: *a flagrant miscarriage of justice*

blew past tense of blow: *The wind blew hard at the coast.*
blue a primary color: *blue sky*

bloc coalition of groups with the same purpose: *a bloc of votes*
block a solid piece of hard material; an obstruction: *block the street*

blond light-colored hair or complexion: *He has blond hair and blue eyes.*
blonde a blond-haired female: *A beautiful blonde stepped onto the stage.*

boar an animal
boor a peasant; a course, rude person: *He is such a boor that I never invite him.*

bore to drill; a wearisome person; past tense of bear: *She bore her pain without complaining.*

board a long thin piece of wood; daily meals as in a boarding house; an official group of people who direct an activity: *board of directors*
bored weary by dullness; fatigued, tired; annoyed: *The story bored me.*

boarder one who pays a stipulated amount for meals and lodging: *My boarder will be leaving at the end of the month.*
border the part of an area that forms its outer boundary; the line that separates one area, state, or country from another; periphery: *They are building a fence along the border.*

bobbin a cylinder or cone for holding thread; a spool or reel
spindle a pin in a spinning wheel used for twisting and winding the thread; a pin bearing the bobbin for a spinning machine; a turned piece of wood used as a banister, chair leg, etc.

bode to be an omen of; to portend: *The future bodes well for you.*
bowed used a bow on a stringed instrument: *bowed a bass violin*

bogey in golf, to score one stroke over par on a hole: *He made a bogey on the last hole.*
boggy wet and spongy; containing bogs: *a boggy field*
bogy a hobgoblin; something that haunts, harasses, or frightens

bold brave, fearless, adventurous, valiant, brazen: *She's bold and flashy.*
bowled past tense of bowl: *She bowled a good game.*

bolder more daring or courageous: *He is far bolder than one would imagine.*
boulder a large rock: *The boulder broke loose and tumbled down the mountain.*

boll   seed pod of a plant, as flax or cotton

bole   tree trunk

bowl   hemispherical vessel; a large wooden ball; a roll of the ball, as in bowling

bootee (also bootie)   a soft knitted slipper or baby shoe

booty   plunder taken from an enemy; stolen or seized goods; a valuable prize or award

born   brought forth by birth: *He was born in a log cabin.*

borne   past participle of the verb *bear*: *She had always borne the burden of responsibility.*

borough   a town or village

burro   small donkey

burrow   hole dug in the ground; to dig a hole

both   the two; not only one: *both shows were canceled*

each   every one of two or more persons or things: *take two books each*; every one individually: *Each one had a different opinion on the matter.*; apiece: *The tickets are four dollars each.*

bough   tree branch: *They hung the swing from the largest bough.*

bow   the front section of a ship or boat; to bend the body, head, or knee as in greeting: *bow to the king*; submit: *bow to a request*

bouillon   a clear, thin broth

bullion   gold or silver in bars, ingots, or plates

boy   a male child

buoy   a floating signal; a life preserver

brace   a clamp; a support for a bodily part; a device that holds something erect

braise   to brown and then cook slowly

braze   to solder metals together

brake   reduce speed; a retarding device: *apply the brakes*

break   separate; destroy; fracture: *break a leg*

brassiere   a woman's undergarment that supports the breasts

brazier   a grill

breach   a violation, as of a law, obligation, or promise: *a breach of trust*

breech   the lower rear portion of a human trunk; buttocks: *a breech birth*

bread   a food; to coat with bread crumbs: *bread the pork chops*

bred   brought about; engendered; raised: *born and bred in Iowa*

breadth   wide scope; width: *she measured the breadth of the fabric*

breath   respiration; a stirring of air: *a breath of spring*

breathe   to inhale and exhale air: *breathe deeply now*; to be alive; to whisper: *Don't breathe a word of this to your mother.*

brews   makes beer, ale, tea, coffee, etc.; concocts, schemes, devises: *brews a plan*

bruise   an injury that does not break the skin but produces a discoloration; contusion; to injure slightly: *bruise someone's feelings*

bridal   pertaining to a bride or a wedding: *She chose a lovely bridal gown.*

bridle   a horse's headgear; to take offense: *She bridled at the implication that she didn't have the right to wear white.*

bring   to carry, convey, or conduct: *I will bring my friend with me when I come.*

fetch   to go, get, and bring back: *My cat plays fetch.*
take   the opposite of bring: *Take me home with you.*

broach   introduce, propose, bring up, submit, advance: *Did you broach the subject at the meeting?*; a cutting tool; a spit for roasting meat
brooch   an ornament having a pin at the back: *That is a lovely brooch on your dress.*

brut   very dry, as champagne
brute   a beast; a brutal person; savage; cruel

burger   hamburger
burgher   citizen of a town or borough

burglary   breaking and entering a building with intent to steal
robbery   taking the property of a person in his or her presence by violence or intimidation
plunder   to rob by open force, as in war; to take wrongfully as by pillage or fraud
theft   the act of stealing; unlawfully taking and carrying away the property of another; larceny

business   an occupation or trade; a concern: *That's none of your business.*; commerce, company: *My business is doing very well.*
busyness   occupied with meaningless activity; the quality of being busy: *Sometimes I get tired of all this busyness.*

but   however, nevertheless, still, except: *She could do nothing but cry.*; on the contrary, yet: *My sister got dessert but it was not what she ordered.*
butt   the end or extremity of anything: *the butt of a pistol*; an end that is not consumed: *a cigarette butt*; a person who is an object of ridicule; a victim, target: *the butt of a joke*; to strike or push with the head or horns: *Goats like to butt their heads against each other.*

buy purchase: *buy a car*; to acquire by exchange or concession; to bribe: *to buy votes*; to accept or believe: *I don't buy that story.*

by next to; close to; *a house by the sea*; through the authority of: *a study by the EPA*; according to: *a lousy movie by anyone's standards*; no later than: *I'm usually home by late afternoon.*

bye secondary matter; side issue; short for *good-bye*; incidentally: *By the bye, how was the dinner?*

C

---

cabal conspiratorial group of plotters; a secret plot or scheme

cable a strong, heavy rope

cache a hiding place; a hidden store of goods: *He had a cache of nonperishable food in case of an invasion.*

cachet an official seal, as on a letter or document; a distinguishing feature: *Courtesy is the cachet of a gracious hostess.*; superior status; prestige: *The diplomatic corps has a certain cachet.*

cash currency or coins: *They'd rather have cash than a credit card.*

caddie a person who carries a golf player's clubs; a rigid wheeled device for moving heavy objects: *a luggage caddie*; to work as a caddie: *I caddie at the country club golf course.*

caddy a container for holding or storing items such as pencils, silverware, food, etc.: *a dessert caddy*

catty malevolent; bitchy; nasty; spiteful: *She made a catty remark about her ex-husband's new girlfriend.*

calendar table showing days, weeks, and months of a year; a list or schedule: *Put the meeting on your calendar.*

calender a machine that presses cloth or paper through rollers: *The laundry used a calender to press the sheets.*

colander a sieve or strainer: *He used a colander to drain the pasta.*

callous   unfeeling; emotionally hardened: *She was so callous that she didn't shed a tear when her husband died.*

callus   a thickening of the horny layer of the skin: *You may have to go to a doctor to get that callus removed.*

Calvary   site of Jesus' crucifixion

cavalry   troops trained to fight in armored vehicles or on horseback

can   to be able to, have the power or skill to: *I can take a bus to the airport. She can paint very well.*

may   to have permission to: *you may go in now;* to express possibility: *The storm may turn into a hurricane.*

canapé   a cracker or thin piece of toast spread with a savory food such as cheese or caviar

canopy   a covering of canvas or other material supported on poles; such as a canopy from a doorway to the curb; an ornamental, rooflike projection

canary   a yellow songbird native to the Canary Islands; a stool pigeon, informer: *The traitor sang like a canary.*

cannery   a place where food is canned: *The cannery produced several thousand cans of food a day.*

candid   frank, ingenuous, outspoken; open and sincere; informal; unposed: *a candid snapshot;*

candied   incrusted with sugar: *candied fruit;* prepared by cooking in sugar: *candied yams;* flattering: *candied words*

cannon   weapon for firing projectiles

canon   law, rule, or code; basis for judgment; criterion

cant   insincere; the private language of the underworld; phraseology peculiar to a particular class or profession: *the cant of the fashion* *industry*; whining or singsong speech, esp. of beggars; hypocrisy, sham, pretense, humbug

can't   contraction of cannot

recant   withdraw or disavow; revoke, rescind, deny: *He recanted his confession.*

canvas   heavy fabric used for making sails; a tent; an oil painting

canvass   to discuss thoroughly; solicit votes; seek opinions; poll: *canvass the neighborhood*

capital   money; principal; city serving as a seat of government; involving death: *capital crime*

capitol   legislature building; also Capitol, meaning the building in which the U.S. Congress meets

carat   the weight of precious stones, especially diamonds: *The stone in her engagement ring was over two carats.*

caret   a writer's and a proofreader's mark: *A caret is a symbol that is used to indicate where material is to be inserted in a document.*

karat   proportion of pure gold used with an alloy: *Her earrings were made of 24 karat gold.*

carbine   a shoulder rifle with a short barrel

carbon   a nonmetallic element

card shark   an expert cardplayer: *He was a card shark who played poker for a living.*

cardsharp   a person who cheats at card games: *Keep your eyes closely on the cardsharp's hands.*

careen   lean or tip to one side while in motion, as car rounding a curve or a ship listing in a storm: *The motorcycle careened around the bend in the road.*

career   move rapidly, go at full speed: *The sports car careered down the highway.*; vocation, lifework, livelihood: *She has made a career of interior decoration.*

caregiver   a person who cares for the sick or disabled: *She is the old man's caregiver.*

caretaker   a person in charge of maintenance or in charge of an estate: *He is the caretaker of the mansion and the grounds.*

caricature   a picture that exaggerates a person's features to produce a comic or grotesque effect: *Political cartoonists often use caricature to illustrate the character of their subject.*

character   distinctive feature or attribute; nature; disposition; makeup: *It is against her character to be anything other than kind.*

caries   decay, as of bone: *dental caries*

carries   conveys or transports from one place to another: *He carries her books home from school.*

carotene   orange fat-soluble pigments found in some plants, such as carrots; vitamin A

keratin   a substance found in the dead outer skin and in horn, hoofs, nails, claws, etc.

carousal   loud, riotous drinking party: *The carousal went on all night long.*

carousel   merry-go-round: *I still remember my first carousel ride when I was a small child.*; a tournament on horseback

cart   a small vehicle pushed or pulled by hand or drawn by a horse or pony: *Don't put the cart before the horse.*

carte   menu, bill of fare; a playing card

carton   a cardboard or plastic box used for storage or shipping: *You will need a carton to pack your dishes in for moving.*

cartoon   a sketch or drawing symbolizing, satirizing, or caricaturing an action, thing, person, or animal: *a cartoon of a political figure*

cast   a group of actors: *the cast for the play was chosen*; mold or pattern; a tinge; to throw forcefully: *cast the first stone*

caste   a class of society; a social status or system: *a caste society*

caster   a small wheel on a swivel: *The grand piano was on casters.*

castor   a bean and the oil derived from it: *Castor beans are very toxic and should not be eaten.*

casual   happening by chance; unexpected; fortuitous: *a casual meeting*; not dressy: *a casual event*

causal   of or implying a cause; relating to or of the nature of cause and effect: *a causal factor*

cataclysm   disaster; a violent upheaval, such as an earthquake; an extensive flood

catechism   a book containing the principles of the Christian religion; a book of instruction in any subject

catch   seize or capture; trap or ensnare; contract, as a cold; a game where a ball is thrown from one person to another

ketch   a sailing vessel with two masts

cause   make, create, produce: *cause a riot*; bring about; a principle or movement to which one is dedicated: *a worthy cause*

caws   the harsh, grating cries of certain birds, such as crows

cede   yield or formally surrender to another: *cede territory*

seed   the ovule of a flowering plant; germ or propagative part of anything: *seed of a rebellion*

ceiling   interior upper surface of a room: *The entryway had a high ceiling.*; a maximum limit; vertical boundary, cloud cover

sealing   using an adhesive agent to close or secure something: *She used sealing wax on the envelope.*

celebrate   to commemorate with festivities: *celebrate a birthday*; honor, laud, applaud: *celebrate a victory*

celibate   a person who abstains from having sex: *She has chosen to be celibate until marriage.*; a person who remains unmarried for religious reasons: *The priests have vowed to remain celibate.*

cell   a small room as in a convent or prison; basic structural unit of all organisms: *a one-celled animal*

sell   to transfer goods or render services in exchange for money: *sell the car*

cellar   a storage room, wholly or partly underground: *They have a wine cellar to keep wine at an appropriate temperature.*

seller   one who sells services, food, merchandise, etc.: *She was the real estate company's top seller.*

censer   a container in which incense is burned: *He lighted the censer on the altar.*

censor   prohibit or restrict the use of something: *They censor motorcycles in the cemetery.*

censure   criticize harshly; reprove; condemn: *He was censured for his use of profanity.*

sensor   a device that detects and responds to a signal or stimulus: *A smoke alarm is an essential sensor in case of fire.*

census   an official enumeration of the population

senses   faculties such as sight, hearing, taste, smell, or touch; sensations; feelings

cents   pennies, bronze coins

scents   odors, perfumes

sense   perceive, grasp, comprehend

since   from then until now; between then and now; before now

cereal   any plant of the grass family yielding an edible grain such as wheat, oats, rice, corn, etc.; a food prepared from grain: *Would you like hot or cold cereal for breakfast?*

serial   consisting of a series: *serial monogamy*; in installments: *magazine serials*

ceremonial   pertaining to a ceremony; formal; ritual: *ceremonial event*

ceremonious   courtly; done with ceremony; elaborately polite: *ceremonious display of friendship*

cession   act of ceding, as of territory

session   a meeting; a period of time

chafe   to irritate: *the starched collar will chafe his neck*; annoy; abrade; to heat by rubbing

chaff   husks of grain; worthless matter: *like chaff in the wind*

chairwoman   presiding officer of a meeting, board, or committee

charwoman   a woman hired to do cleaning

champagne   sparkling wine; a pale yellow-gray

champaign   level and open country

chance   luck or fortune; a risk or hazard; accident; fortuity: *We meet, not really by chance.*

chants   psalms, canticles, or songs that are sung in a rhythmic, monotonous tone: *chants of a bird*

chard   a variety of beet with leaves that are used as a vegetable

charred   burned or reduced to charcoal; scorched; singed

chased   pursued; driven or expelled by force or harassment: *chased out of the house*

chaste virgin; celibate; undefiled; pure in style; simple: *a chaste design*

cheap not expensive; poor; shoddy
cheep to chirp or peep

cheek either side of a face; nerve, audacity, gall, impudence: *the kid has a lot of cheek*
chic fashionable, stylish; style and elegance, smart, modish: *she looks so chic in that black dress*
chick young chicken or other bird; a child; a young pretty woman
sheik a Muslim religious official; a leader of an Arab family, village, or tribe

chews grinds and bites with the teeth; masticates: *He chews with his mouth open.*
choose opt; pick out; select: *She will not choose him as a dinner partner again.*

childish immature; infantile: *Screaming and stamping your feet is childish.*
childlike like or befitting a child; innocent: *His childlike bashfulness is charming.*

choir a group of singers, esp. in a church service; a group of musicians: *a string choir*
quire a set of twenty-four uniform sheets of paper

choral sung by or adapted for a chorus or choir
chorale harmonized hymn; a chorus or choir
coral hard, rocklike structures formed by marine coelenterates; yellowish red
corral an enclosure for livestock

chord   three or more musical tones
cord   a small rope; trousers made of corduroy
cored   removed the center of a fruit

choreography   the art of arranging the movements, steps, and patterns of
    dancers
chorography   a systematic, description and analysis of a region

chronical   having long duration, as of a disease: *a chronical condition*
chronicle   chronological record of events; recount, relate, report

chute   an inclined tube, trough, or shaft for conveying water, grain, etc. to a
    lower level; parachute
shoot   to hit with a missile discharged from a weapon; to project, impel,
    hurl, cast, or throw

cite   to quote; refer to as an example; commend; summon before a court of
    law
sight   vision; a view; mental perception; prospect; something worth seeing
site   position; location; place; setting of an event

clamber   climb with hands and feet: *She clambered up the boulders.*
clammer   one who gathers or digs clams
clamor   loud noise; a protest; demand: *The clamor was tumultuous.*

clause   group of words; provision in a document
claws   sharp, curved nails on an animal

clef   in music, a symbol on a staff showing the pitch of the notes
cleft   split; divided; a crack or crevice; an indentation between two parts, as of
    the chin

clench   grip tightly: *Clench the tool firmly in your hand.*; bring together, as teeth: *She spoke through clenched teeth.*

clinch   secure; settle: *clinch the deal*; hold, as in boxing: *The fighters were in a clinch.*

click   a brief, sharp sound: *The click of her heels was heard on the stairs.*; to press a computer button: *click on "open"*

clique   exclusive group of friends or associates: *The members formed a clique.*

climactic   pertaining to or coming to a climax: *a climactic second act*

climacteric   menopause; any critical period: *a climacteric of civil unrest*

climatic   pertaining to climate; a prevailing condition or atmosphere: *The plane was grounded due to unfavorable climatic conditions.*

climb   to go up; ascend: *climb the stairs*, mount, scale: *climb a mountain*

clime   climate, weather; mood, atmosphere, tone: *The argument made for a tense clime.*

close   to shut; bring to an end: *It's time to close the meeting.*

clothes   wearing apparel; garments: *Choose the proper clothes for the occasion.*

closer   a person or thing that closes: *She was called in to be the closer of the deal.*; nearer: *She's closer to understanding the situation.*

closure   the act of closing; bringing to an end; something that closes: *The arrest brought closure to the difficult case.*

cloture   a method of closing a debate and forcing an immediate vote

coal   a combustible mineral used as fuel: *They used coal for heating their homes.*

cole   cabbage or rape plant: *cole slaw*

kohl   a preparation used as eye makeup: *She accented her eyes with kohl.*

coarse   lacking delicacy or refinement; crude; harsh; rough; boorish; gross: *His language was coarse and unsuitable for children to hear.*

course   route or path; progress; duration; a way of behaving: *She chose the wisest course.*

coaster   a coasting sled or toboggan; a vessel engaged in coastal trade; a disk placed under an object to protect the surface below: *Please place a coaster under your glass.*

costar   an actor or actress who shares star billing with another; a performer whose status is slightly below that of a star: *She is the costar of the film.* (also co-star)

coat   an outer garment extending to the waist or below: *This coat will keep you warm.*; the fur of an animal: *The fox has a beautiful coat.*; a layer of covering material: *The fence needs another coat of paint.*

cote   a small shed or shelter for sheep or birds; a cottage or hut: *The cote was made of logs and had only two rooms.*

coca   a South American tree with leaves that contain cocaine

coco   coconut or coconut palm

cocoa   powder made from cacao seeds, a hot drink made from cocoa powder and milk

coddle   treat tenderly; pamper; indulge; baby

cuddle   hug affectionately; to lie close and snug; embrace

collage   an artwork created by pasting on a surface various materials such as magazine clippings, photographs, tickets, and other items not normally associated with each other

college   an institution of higher learning

collision   the act of colliding; a crash: *Traffic was tied up due to a collision on the freeway.*

collusion   a secret agreement to defraud or deceive: *Proof of collusion led to their arrest.*

colloquial not formal or literary; belonging to or typical of ordinary or familiar language

colloquium an academic conference or seminar

colloquy the act of conversing; a conversation

coma deep prolonged unconsciousness

comma punctuation mark (,) that indicates a pause in a sentence: *A misplaced comma can convey a very different meaning.*

command to direct with authority; order, bid, demand, govern, lead: *command the troops*

commend to praise as worthy; to entrust, acclaim, laud: *They commend his leadership ability.*

commence originate, inaugurate, begin, start: *commence the show*

comments remarks; observations, annotations, criticisms: *There were harsh comments on the performance.*

compare to liken; relate; examine similarities: *compare the shades of blue*

contrast to examine differences; a striking exhibition of unlikeness: *The contrast of styles intensified the impact of the paintings.*

compartment a space partitioned off; a separate room or section: *baggage compartment*; a separate function; division

comportment personal bearing or conduct; demeanor; behavior: *His comportment was above reproach.*

compassion a deep sympathy for the sorrows of others, with an urge to alleviate their pain: *The nurse showed great compassion for the injured children.*

empathy ability to imagine oneself in the condition of another; a vicarious participation in another's emotions: *The widow expressed empathy for the woman who had just lost her husband.*

sympathy a general kinship with another's feelings no matter of what kind: *He sent a sympathy card to the widow.*

complacent   self-satisfied; smug; unbothered: *He is too complacent to make changes.*

complaisant   eager to please; deferential; obliging; agreeable or gracious: *He is a complaisant host.*

compliant   inclined to act in accord with the rules; acquiescent: *She has a compliant disposition.*

compleat   highly skilled and accomplished in all aspects: *The compleat writer is adept in many genres.*

complete   finished, ended, concluded; having all parts or elements: *a complete set of encyclopedias*

complement   something that completes or brings to perfection: *Wine complements a dinner.*

compliment   an expression of admiration; praise; regards: *My compliments to the chef.*

compose   create or put together; constitute; to calm one's mind or body: *After the accident, it took me a long time to compose myself.*

comprise   to include all; contain: *Fifty states comprise the Union.*

composer   one who writes music: *Bach was a great composer.*

composure   calmness; tranquility; serenity; coolness; self-possession: *She maintained her composure during her entire performance.*

comprehensible   capable of being understood; intelligible: *a comprehensible explanation of a scientific study*

comprehensive   of large scope; inclusive; having an extended mental range or grasp: *a comprehensive study of the situation*

compulsion   an irresistible impulse; coercion: *She couldn't fight her compulsion to buy things she didn't need.*

compunction   regret; contrition; remorse: *She felt no compunction about taking what didn't belong to her.*

concord goodwill, friendship; a treaty; compact; covenant; agreement: *in concord with a decision*

conquered subdued; overcame by force; gained victory over; mastered: *I came, I saw, I conquered.*

conducive contribute to a result; tending to bring about or cause: *A well-balanced diet is conducive to good health.*

conductive managerial; directive

confidant a friend to whom secrets are confided (*fem.* confidante)

confident having strong belief; sure; certain; self-assured

confidentially privately, intimately, secretly: *Confidentially, I believe they are having an affair.*

confidently with assurance, with certainty, boldly: *I can say confidently that they are having an affair.*

confirmation verification: *receive an e-mail confirmation for an order placed online*; a religious rite or ceremony: *Her whole family attended her confirmation.*

conformation symmetrical arrangement of parts: *The conformation of the structure was very pleasing.*

connote imply in addition to the literal meaning; intimate: *Home cooking connotes comfort food.*

denote be a sign of; convey; stand as a name for; indicate: *A fever may denote an infection.*

conscience recognition of difference between right and wrong: *His conscience bothered him when he cheated on the test.*

conscious aware; capable of thought or will: *a conscious decision*; cognizant: *She was conscious of the stranger standing close to her.*

conservation   controlled use and protection of natural resources, as forests, wetlands, endangered species, etc.

conversation   talk; spoken exchange of ideas, feelings, thoughts, and opinions

conservationist   an advocate of the protection of natural resources: *The conservationist lobbied to save the trees.*

conservative   one who favors traditional views and values: *She dresses in a conservative style.*

conservator   one who is responsible for a person ruled incompetent: *His son became his conservator.*

consul   a diplomat residing in a foreign country: *the American consul in France*

council   a gathering of people for consultation: *The matter was brought before the council for an opinion.*

counsel   consultation; a lawyer; advice; guidance: *She sought counsel for the proposed adoption.*

consular   (as in consular agent) a consular officer of the lowest rank stationed where no full consular service is established

consulate   the premises officially occupied by a consul; the position, authority or term of service of a consul

councilor   a member of a council

counselor   an advisor; a lawyer; an official of an embassy who ranks below an ambassador or minister

[The above words are not interchangeable. *A council* is an assembly of persons who make deliberations and offer advice. A member of such a group is a *councilor. Counsel* means advice given to another. A person who gives the advice is a *counselor.*]

contagious   transmissible by contact; catching; capable of carrying disease: *A head cold can be contagious.*

infectious   capable of causing infection; transmitted without contact: *Cholera is an infectious epidemic disease caused by a microorganism.*

continual   intermittent; often repeated: *continual chiming of a clock*
continuous   uninterrupted in time: *continuous ticking of a clock*

[These words are often used without any distinction in meaning, as are *continually* and *continuously.* To make a clear distinction, use the contrasting terms *intermittent* and *uninterrupted.*]

convey   to carry; move; take from one place to another; transport; communicate; make known
convoy   to accompany or escort; a ship, fleet, group of vehicles, etc.; accompanied by a protecting escort

coop   an enclosure or cage: *a chicken coop*; a co-op: *They bought their food at a co-op.*
coup   (*koo*) a brilliant stratagem; overturn; upset: *His win was quite a coup.*
coupe   a closed two-door car; a frozen dessert: *She chose the coupe rather than the sedan.*

coot   a dark gray aquatic bird; a foolish person: *He's just an old coot.*
cute   attractive in a dainty way; pleasingly pretty: *a cute puppy*; affectedly clever; precious: *too old to be acting so unbearably cute*

core   central part: *apple core*; heart: *rotten to the core*
corps   body of persons; a military unit: *a loyal member of the corps*
corpse   dead body

corespondent   a person charged with committing adultery with the defendant in a divorce suit
correspondent   one who communicates through letters; one employed by a news agency to supply news or articles from a remote location

corner   the place where two converging lines or surfaces meet; an end; margin; edge

coroner   an officer who investigates by inquest any death not clearly resulting from natural causes

corporal   of the body: *corporal punishment*; non-commissioned officer

corporeal   of a material nature; tangible: *corporeal evidence*

cosign   to sign a document jointly with another; to endorse, as for a mortgage: *his father cosigned the loan on his new car*

cosine   a mathematical term

costume   a style of clothing typical of a particular time, country, or people; a set of clothes appropriate for a particular occasion: *a Halloween costume*

custom   a practice followed as a matter of course among a people; a habitual practice of an individual: *It is her custom to take a walk every night before dinner.*

courier   messenger, esp. one on a diplomatic mission

currier   a person who tans hides

courtesy   politeness, kindness, consideration

curtsy   a girl's or woman's formal greeting made by bending the knees and lowering the body

coward   a person who lacks courage; very fearful or timid; craven; dastard: *She was too much of a coward to go out after dark.*

cowered   cringed, recoiled, crouched as in fear: *The puppy cowered in the corner.*

creak   a squeaking or grating sound: *The floorboards creak.*

creek   a small stream: *A creek runs through the property.*

credible plausible, likely, reasonable; believable or worthy of belief: *a credible argument*

creditable bringing credit or honor; praiseworthy; meritorious; estimable: *a fine person of creditable character*

crevasse a deep cleft in glacial ice, chasm; a breach in a river levee

crevice a fissure or crack forming an opening

crewel worsted yarn for embroidery and edging

cruel willfully causing pain or distress; merciless

critic one who censures; a person who reviews literary, artistic, or musical works, etc.: *The critic gave a rave review of the play.*

critique a critical essay or analysis; an instance of formal criticism: *The critique was devastating.*

crone a withered old woman

crony a close friend or companion

croquet outdoor game using wooden balls and long-handled mallets

croquette small patty or cake of minced food coated with bread crumbs and deep-fried

crumble disintegrate; to break into crumbs

crumple collapse; to crush together or press into wrinkles: *She crumpled the paper and threw it away.*

cruise to fly, drive, or sail at a constant speed: *cruise along the highway*

cruse earthen pot or bottle for liquids

cubical cubic; of or relating to volume

cubicle small sleeping compartment; small partitioned space

cue   hint; prompting: *The actor was given his cue.*
queue   waiting line of people or cars: *There was a long queue at the movies.*

curios   unusual objects of art, valued as a curiosity: *She has a special cabinet for her curios.*
curious   eager to acquire knowledge; inquisitive: *He was curious to know how she had come by so many of the rare objects.*

currant   small dried seedless grape
current   belonging to the present time; steady movement of water; flow of electric charge

currently   at the present time: *She is currently working on her thesis.*
presently   in a little while, soon, shortly: *The supervisor will be back presently.*

cymbal   brass plate used as a percussion instrument: *the crashing of the cymbals*
symbol   a sign; something that represents something else: *A dove is a symbol of peace.*

D

---

dab   to press briefly with a cloth, sponge, etc. without rubbing: *dab a cut to stop the bleeding*; to press lightly
daub   to coat or smear a surface with a thick substance; to paint crudely: *daub the primer on the raw wood*

dabble   spatter or splash; undertake an activity casually: *dabble in politics*
dapple   mottled or spotted marking, as on a horse; to mark with spots

daily   occurring every day: regularly, constantly: *he gets a newspaper daily*

dally   delay; waste time: *dally along the way*; play about; flirt: *dally with her affections*

dairy   a place where milk and cream are kept and butter and cheese are made; a shop or company that sells milk, butter, etc.
diary   a private daily record of one's experiences and feelings; journal, daybook, log, chronicle

dam   a barrier built to hold back water and raise its level; block up; obstruct: *The beaver's dam caused the field to flood.*
damn   an uttered curse; to doom to hell; condemn; censure: *Damn the act, not the person.*; commend without enthusiasm: *damn with faint praise*; a bit: *not worth a damn*

dandle   to lightly bounce a child on one's knee or in one's arms; pamper; pet
dangle   suspend loosely and sway to and fro: *dangle the wind chimes from the tree branch*; to hold out a hope enticingly: *dangle the prize in front of the contestant*

days   plural of day: *There are seven days in a week.*
daze   to stun with a blow: *The attack left him in a daze.*; to overwhelm; astound; dumbfound; flabbergast: *Daze them with your sleight of hand.*

deal   apportion; deliver; distribute playing cards; a bargain: *What a deal!*
dele   to take out or delete

dear   beloved, cherished; greatly valued: *The old photographs are dear to her.*
deer   hoofed ruminant mammal: *The deer stood motionless in the forest.*

decedent   a dead person: *The decedent was given a proper burial.*
descendant   a person or animal that is descended from a specific ancestor; an offspring: *a descendant of the early settlers*

deceased   no longer living; dead
diseased   infirm; inflicted with a disease

decimate   to destroy a great number or proportion of: *Cholera decimated the city's population*; to select by lot and kill every tenth person
destroy   demolish; ruin; annihilate; kill, slay; defeat completely: *They will destroy the entire village.*

decree   a formal and authoritative order having the force of law: *a presidential decree*; a judicial decision or order; a doctrinal act of an ecumenical council
degree   a mark, grade, level, phase; any of a series of steps or stages, as in a process or course of action; a point in any scale; extent, measure, scope, or the like: *To what degree is he willing to cooperate?*

deduce   infer; draw a logical conclusion: *I deduce that you are in agreement.*
deduct   subtract; take away from: *I deduct my expenses.*

deference   courteous respect for another's opinion, wishes, or judgment: *treated with deference*
difference   disparity; unlikeness; distinction: *made a difference*

deferential   courteous, dutiful, respectful: *She assumed a deferential attitude toward her teacher.*
differential   pertaining to diversity; distinctive: *a differential feature*; a gear in a vehicle

definite   precise; exact; positive; certain: *a definite decision*; specific: *a definite time*; particular; well-defined
definitive   reliable; complete: *the definitive works of Shakespeare*; satisfying all criteria: *a definitive scientific study*; absolute, ultimate, supreme

defuse   to remove the fuse from; to make less dangerous or tense: *His apology defused a potentially ugly situation.*

diffuse   to pour out and spread; to scatter widely or thinly; disseminate: *diffuse the seeds*

delusion   a persistent false belief: *A paranoiac has delusions of persecution.*
illusion   misinterpretation of things that exist: *A mirage is an illusion caused by atmospheric conditions.*

demur   to make objection, esp. on the grounds of scruples; take exception; hesitation
demure   shy; modest; reserved; retiring

dependence   reliance; confidence; trust: *dependence on a person's honesty*; conditional or contingent on something: *dependence on the outcome of the trial*; the state of being dependent: *drug dependence*
dependents   persons who depend on someone or something for aid or support: *She has six dependents.*

depose   to remove from office or position: *It took a revolution to depose the king.*; to give sworn testimony in writing: *to depose that it was true*
depots   railroad or bus stations; terminals; storehouses

deposition   removal from an office or position; the process of depositing: *deposition of the documents with the Library of Congress*; the giving of testimony under oath; a statement to be used in court in place of the spoken testimony of the witness
disposition   natural mental and emotional outlook or mood; characteristic attitude: *has a mean disposition*; an inclination: *a gambling disposition*; the final settlement of a matter

deprave   to make morally bad or evil
deprive   to withhold something from another; strip, divest

depravation   corruption; evil-doing
deprivation   without economic or social necessities; dispossession; loss

deprecate   express disapproval of; deplore, belittle, denounce, condemn: *deprecate a criminal*

depreciate   lessen the value or price of; downgrade, disparage, minimize: *depreciate a car*

descendant   one descended from an ancestor

descendent   moving downward

descent   downward incline or passage: *a steep descent*

dissent   to differ in sentiment or opinion; disapproval; disagreement: *open dissent*

desert   a dry, barren region: *Mojave Desert*; deserved: *received his just desert*; abandon: *desert a family to pursue selfish desires*

dessert   sweet food, often served as the last course of a meal: *I'll have my dessert first.*

desolate   barren, devastated: *a treeless, desolate landscape*; deserted; uninhabited; solitary; lonely; feeling abandoned by friends or by hope; forlorn; dismal; gloomy: *desolate prospects*

dissolute   indifferent to moral restraints; given to immoral or improper conduct; licentious; dissipated; corrupt, loose, debauched, wanton: *dissolute actions of a person with no conscience*

desperate   rash, frantic, hopeless, desolate: *The situation seemed desperate.*

disparate   separate, divergent, unlike: *disparate objectives of the two groups*

detract   to take away a part of the quality, value, or reputation: *Don't detract from the value of his remarks.*

distract   to disturb or trouble greatly: *Her grief distracted her from her work.*; bewilder, agitate, pain, torment, distress; to provide a pleasant diversion for; amuse; entertain: *A good movie will always distract me from my worries.*

device   a crafty scheme; gadget; design; ruse: *His friendliness was only a device to gain your trust.*

devise   contrive, plan, or elaborate; form a plan; prepare: *He will devise a way to get your money.*

dew   condensed moisture: *The early morning dew was on the meadow.*

do   to perform an act, duty, or role: *Do nothing until you hear from me.*; to accomplish; finish; complete: *Do your homework.*; to exert oneself: *Do your best*; to deal with, fix, clean: *Do the dishes.*

due   owed at present: *This bill is due now.*; owed at a later time: *This bill is due next month.*; owing as a moral or natural right: *You're due for a reward in heaven.*; rightful; proper; fitting: *due care*

diagram   a chart, plan, or scheme

diaphragm   the partition separating the thoracic cavity from the abdominal cavity in mammals; a contraceptive device worn by a female over the uterine cervix during sexual intercourse

dialectal   of a dialect

dialectic   of logical argumentation

dieing   cutting, forming, or stamping with a die

dyeing   coloring materials with dye

dying   about to expire; drawing to a close

different   dissimilar; unlike; separate and distinct

diffident   hesitant to assert oneself; timid

dinghy   a small boat

dingy   dirty-looking; drab

disapprove   withhold approval from; refuse to sanction; deplore; criticize

disprove   refute; invalidate; discredit, negate, confute

disassemble   take to pieces; take apart
dissemble   talk or act hypocritically; disguise or conceal

disburse   pay out; spend
dispense   distribute in portions or parts; administer; release or exempt
disperse   scatter; dissipate; spray; dispel

discomfit   thwart; confuse; frustrate; disconcert
discomfort   physical or mental distress

discreet   judicious in one's conduct or speech; careful; circumspect;
   prudent; modest
discrete   constituting a separate thing; distinct; different; individual;
   unconnected

discus   a disk thrown in athletic competitions
discuss   talk over; examine a subject

disinterested   unbiased by personal interest; not influenced by selfish
   motives; impartial; neutral
uninterested   not interested, uncaring, apathetic, indifferent

dissidence   disagreement, dissent
dissonance   discord, conflict, a harsh or unpleasant combination of sounds

divers   several, various, sundry: *The artist used divers articles in her collage.*
diverse   unlike in kind; distinct; separate; divergent: *There were diverse
   beliefs among the parishioners.*

doe   the female of a deer or related animal
dough   a thick mixture of flour or meal

doggy a small dog
dogie or dogy a stray or motherless calf

done finished: *all done for the day*; cooked completely: *Soup's done.*
dun a demand for payment

dual made up of two parts; for two; double
duel a prearranged combat between two people

E

---

earn to acquire by effort: *earn a living*
urn a vessel or vase

earthly earthbound; worldly: *earthly goods*; mortal; mundane: *earthly affairs*
earthy unrefined: *an earthy smell*; realistic; practical; lusty: *Mae West was known for her earthy sense of humor.*

eaves projecting overhang of a roof
eves days or nights preceding a holiday

eclipse the obscuring of the light from one celestial body by the passage of another between it and the observer: *lunar eclipse; solar eclipse*; a sudden loss of importance in relation to a newly arrived person or thing: *The status of the lead actress was eclipsed by a young ingénue in the film.*
elapse the passage or termination of a period of time: *Eight hours have elapsed since we ate.*
ellipsis a set of three dots indicating an omission in a text: *A foolish . . . is the hobgoblin of little minds.*

either one or the other: *It's either too hot or too cold.*
ether an anesthetic; the upper regions of space; the heavens

elegy   a mournful or melancholy musical composition or poem written as a lament for one who is dead: *The organist played a beautiful elegy at the memorial service.*

eulogy   an oral or written laudatory tribute; a set oration in honor of a deceased person; high praise or commendation: *The minister gave a touching eulogy at the funeral.*

elicit   to draw or bring out; educe; evoke: *Your story elicits memories of my childhood.*

illicit   not legally permitted; unlicensed; unlawful: *Illicit drugs are rampant in the city.*

eligible   worthy of choice; desirable: *an eligible bachelor*; meeting the requirement: *eligible for parole*; legally qualified to be elected to office: *eligible for the presidency*; suitable, fitting

illegible   impossible or hard to read because of poor handwriting or faded print: *an illegible document*

elocution   the art of public speaking, emphasizing gesture, vocal production, and delivery; public speaking style: *His elocution was powerful and persuasive.*

eloquence   fluent and persuasive discourse: *She speaks with such eloquence.*

elucidation   clarification; making clear: *Your method requires elucidation.*

elusive   hard to express: *an elusive concept*; cleverly evasive: *an elusive con man*; tricky, slippery, shifty, baffling

illusive   deceptive, misleading; of the nature of an illusion; unreal; false; imaginary; fancied: *an illusive appearance of the deceased during a séance.*

emanate   to flow out, issue, or proceed; come forth; originate; emit; arise, spring: *His great talent emanates from the very depths of his being.*

eminent   prominent; distinguished; noteworthy: *an eminent author*

immanent   innate, inborn, intrinsic: *an immanent gift of musical ability*; inherent; existing or remaining within; subjective

imminent   about to occur at any moment; impending: *in imminent danger*

emerge   to come into view; emanate: *Watch carefully and you will see the image emerge.*

immerge   to plunge, as into a fluid; to disappear, as the moon in the shadow of the sun: *The whale immerged back into the sea.*

emigrant   expatriate; one who emigrates

immigrant   person who comes to a country of which he is not a citizen; a migrant

emigrate   migrate; to leave a country to live elsewhere: *to emigrate from England to the United States*

immigrate   enter a country of which one is not a native; introduce as settlers: *immigrate cheap labor*

empiric   a person who depends on experience or observation alone; a quack; charlatan

empirical   verifiable: *empirical evidence*; practical; pragmatic; derived from or guided by experience or experiment

empress   a woman who rules an empire; the wife or widow of an emperor

impress   to apply pressure; to affect or influence strongly; to compel someone to serve in the military

emulate   to strive to equal or excel; to vie with successfully

imitate   to copy the actions, appearance, or mannerisms of another; ape, mimic, mock, parody

energize   give energy to; to put out energy: *A brisk walk in the cold air will energize you.*

enervate   deprive of vitality; weaken: *Constant worry will enervate you.*

invigorate   give vigor, vitality, or strength: *Weight-lifting will invigorate you.*

enfold   to wrap up; envelop; to surround as if with folds: *enfolded in* *mystery*; embrace: *enfolded in her lover's arms*

unfold   to become clear, apparent, or known: *the mystery unfolds slowly*; to spread or open out: *unfold the blanket*; to lay open to view; to set forth; explain; to develop

engross   involve, immerse, engage; to occupy completely: *Their jobs engross them.*; absorb: *She is engrossed in her novel.*; to write in a clear, formal manner, as a public document: *to engross a deed*; to monopolize

engulf   envelope, bury, inundate, deluge, swamp; to swallow up in a gulf; submerge: *The flood engulfed all the low-lying houses.*

ensure   to secure or guarantee; safeguard; make sure or certain: *take measures to ensure success*

insure   warrant; protect against loss; to issue an insurance policy: *Will this insure me in the event of a natural disaster?*

enter   to come or go into; penetrate: *enter a room; enter the bloodstream*

inter   place in a grave or tomb: *They will inter him tomorrow.*

intern   to restrict or confine within prescribed limits, as prisoners of war: *They will intern the prisoners at the camp for at least a month.*

entomology   scientific study of insects

etymology   study of the history of words

entrepreneur   one who organizes and manages an enterprise; one who owns and runs his own business; an independent contractor

intrapreneur   an employee of a corporation who has the freedom and financial support to create new products, services, or systems for the corporation without having to follow its protocols

envelop   to wrap around; enfold; hide; enclose: *Envelop the area with high walls.*

envelope   a flat paper cover or wrapper: *Put the letter into an envelope.*

ephemeral   lasting a short time; transitory; short-lived: *It was an ephemeral but delightful visit.*

ethereal   intangible; delicate; heavenly; spiritual: *It was an ethereal visitation by someone from another world.*

envy   a feeling of discontent or covetousness of another's advantages, possessions, or attainments; desire for something possessed by another: *I envy her talent for decorating.*

jealousy   jealous resentment against a person enjoying success or advantage; anger or fear of losing something or someone to a rival: *Her unbridled jealousy is apparent whenever her boyfriend dances with another woman.*

[Although *envy* and *jealousy* are close in meaning, they have some different connotations. To *envy* is to feel unhappy because someone else possesses or has accomplished something you wish you had yourself. *Jealousy* is resenting someone who has gained something that you think you more rightly deserve. It also refers to the anguish caused by fear or suspicions of unfaithfulness.]

epigram   witticism, quip; ingenious saying tersely expressed

epigraph   an inscription on a building or statue; quotation at the beginning of a book or chapter

epitaph   inscription on a tomb or mortuary monument; words in praise of the deceased

epithet   a word or phrase applied to a person to describe a quality; nickname; sobriquet; designation; a curse or insult

equable   uniform; free from changes or variations

equatable   regarded, treated, or represented as equivalent

equitable   characterized by fairness; just and right; impartial; unbiased

erasable   capable of being rubbed out; easily erased: *Write in pencil so that it is erasable.*

irascible   easily provoked, testy, touchy, short-tempered: *an irascible boss; an irascible response*

erase   remove, as by rubbing or wiping out
delete   to strike out or cancel, as from a text

eraser   something used to erase, as writing in pencil
erasure   an act of erasing

eruption   sudden, violent outburst; ejection of molten rock or steam from a volcano or geyser
irruption   a breaking or bursting in; a violent incursion or invasion

especially   chiefly, particularly: *Winter is especially hard on older people.*
specially   specifically: *The dress was specially designed for the occasion.*

espouse   adopt; champion, advocate: *espouse a plan*; to marry
expound   explain; state in detail: *to expound a theory*

ethic   system of moral principles or values
ethnic   relating to a religious, racial, or cultural group

euphemize   to substitute a mild expression for one thought to be offensive: using *to pass air* instead of *to fart*
euthanize   put to death painlessly or allow to die rather than to suffer from an incurable and painful condition: *The vet had to euthanize my terminally ill cat.*

every man   each man, all men
everyman   an ordinary person representative of humanity; an ordinary man representative of all men

every woman   each woman, all women
everywoman   an ordinary woman representative of all women

every day   each day: *He brings me the paper every day.*
everyday   ordinary, commonplace, usual: *an everyday occurrence*

evoke   to elicit: *His speech will evoke protests*; reawaken: *to evoke a memory*
invoke   to make supplication; to declare to be binding: *to invoke the rules*

ewe   a female sheep
yew   an evergreen tree having needlelike or scalelike
foliage
you   the pronoun of the second-person singular or plural: *You may come with me. This is for you.*

exacerbate   intensify; worsen; inflame; increase the severity of: *Her response only exacerbated the situation.*
exasperate   annoy extremely; incense; vex; anger: *She was exasperated by the noisy neighbors.*

exalt   praise; elevate; glorify; ennoble
exult   rejoice exceedingly; delight; revel

exercise   physical, mental, or spiritual activity
exorcise   to expel an evil spirit

expand   extend, swell, enlarge; spread out: *It will expand its wings and fly away.*
expend   use up: *expend energy*; pay out; disburse; consume, empty

expansive   comprehensive; extensive; effusive; sociable, extroverted, outgoing, unreserved: *She has an expansive personality.*

expensive   very high-priced; costly: *an expensive gown*

explicate   to unfold; to make the meaning clear, explain: *explicate a theory*
implicate   to connect or involve incriminatingly: *implicate a witness*; to
   imply: *implicate that someone is guilty*

explicit   clearly expressed; leaving nothing implied; unequivocal: *explicit*
   instructions; outspoken,
   precise
implicit   implied rather than expressly stated: *an implicit agreement*;
   absolute: *implicit trust*; inherent

extant   still existing; not destroyed: *There is only one extant copy of the book.*
extent   range; distance; measure; length; degree: *He is agreeable to some*
   extent.
extinct   no longer in use; no longer existing: *Many animals are now extinct.*

eyelet   a small hole as in cloth or leather for ornamental effect; grommet
islet   a very small island

F

---

fabrication   manufacture; something fabricated; an untruthful statement:
   His alibi was a total fabrication.
fib   a small or trivial lie; minor falsehood: *He meant no harm; it was only a*
   fib.

facet   a small polished surface of a cut gem; aspect; phase; side: *Consider*
   every facet of the argument.
faucet   a device for controlling the flow of liquid from a pipe by opening or
   closing it; a tap or spigot: *You'll need a plumber to fix that leaky faucet.*

facetious   not to be taken seriously; amusing; humorous; frivolous: *I was* *only being facetious.*

factitious artificial; contrived: *His enthusiastic response was factitious.*; made; manufactured: *a factitious part*

fictitious spurious, fake; fictional; created or assumed with the intention to conceal: *a fictitious name*; imaginatively produced: *a fictitious story*

facilitation making easy or less difficult; assisting the progress of: *The facilitation of your move will be made by the students.*

felicitation congratulation; an expression of good wishes: *Felicitations on your graduation.*

facility something that serves a specific function: *a parking facility*; an easy-flowing manner: *facility of style*; skill, aptitude, or dexterity: *He has a great facility with words.*

felicity great happiness; bliss; a skillful faculty: *Her felicity of expression is delightful.*

faction discord, disagreement, schism, split, friction; a group or clique within a larger group: *A faction in the government wants to rewrite the Constitution.*; dissension: *a time of faction and strife*

fiction literature consisting of imaginative stories and characters, as novels and short stories: *Her book is a work of fiction.*; the act of feigning, inventing, or imagining; fable, fantasy

faint swoon: *The horrible news made her faint.*; feeble; timid; dim: *a faint light in the distance*

feint a misleading movement: *feint a pass*; a pretense

fair just; light in color; moderately good; an exhibition

fare to get along; food; cost of transportation

faker one who produces counterfeits; swindler; fraud

fakir Muslim religious mendicant; Hindu ascetic; beggar; one who performs feats of magic

fallow   marked by inactivity; plowed unseeded land: *They let the land go fallow for a season.*

follow   to go after; pursue; obey: *follow one's instincts*

fame   widespread reputation, esp. of a favorable character; renown; public eminence: *His fame as a writer grew with each novel he wrote.*

notability   distinction, prominence: *She is a doctor of great notability.*

notoriety   shame; infamy; disrepute; known widely and unfavorably: *The extensive news coverage of his trial for murdering his wife brought him notoriety.*

familial   pertaining to a family: *familial ties*; heredity: *a familial disease*

familiar   generally known: *a familiar plant*; informal: *to write in a familiar style*; personal; intimate: *a familiar friend*

farther   at or to a greater distance, degree, or extent: *the farther side of the building*

further   furthermore; in addition: *further, he even brought a friend*; help or advance the progress of: *She will further her own career.*

[*Farther* and *further* have been used interchangeably throughout their histories. However, only *further* should be used to mean *moreover, furthermore, additionally,* or *to advance the progress of.*]

fate   karma; destiny; chance; luck: *We met through a lucky twist of fate.*

fete   a day of celebration; a holiday: *It was a joyous fete.*

faun   a woodland deity

fawn   a young deer; to court favor

fay   a fairy

fey   fated to die soon; under a spell; enchanted; whimsical; otherworldly

faze   to worry or disturb: *The ghost story didn't faze the children.*

phase a stage in development: *The toddler is just going through a phase.*

feat achievement; exploit; courageous, daring act: *an extraordinary feat*
feet plural of foot: *feet firmly planted on the ground*

ferment agitation; unrest; excitement: *The city was in the grip of political ferment.*
foment incite; instigate rebellion: *to foment a riot.*

feudal relating to lands held in fee: *a feudal estate*
futile ineffectual; useless; incapable of producing any result; not successful: *Trying to get the horse to drink water was futile.*

fewer of a smaller number: *He said the same thing, but in fewer words.*
less to a smaller extent, amount, or degree: *He was less than courteous.*

[*Few* and *fewer* should be used only before a plural: *a few cookies remained; fewer people attended. Less* should modify only singular nouns: *less money, less courage.* When a plural noun suggests a combination into a unit, *less* is used: *less than fifteen cents* [a sum of money]; *less than fifteen miles* (a unit of distance); *less sugar* (a mass noun).]

finale the concluding part of a performance or proceeding; the last movement of a concert, opera, or composition: *The finale was the most exciting part of the symphony.*
finality conclusiveness or decisiveness; something that is final; an ultimate act: *She slammed the door behind her with finality.*

finally in the end; at last; eventually; after considerable delay: *After many attempts, she finally got it right.*
finely elegantly; delicately; minutely; nicely; subtly; excellently: *a finely crafted story*; in fine particles or pieces: *finely chopped apples*

find   discover; come upon by chance; obtain by search or effort: *find a four-leaf clover*; achieve, win, earn, acquire: *find an apartment*

fined   penalized for an offense: *He was fined $50 for parking in a handicapped zone.*

fineness   state of being fine; superior quality; proportion of pure precious metal in an alloy: *The fineness of the diamond was extraordinary.*

finesse   extreme delicacy in performance; skill; adroitness; trick or stratagem; skill in handling a highly sensitive situation; adroit and artful management: *exceptional diplomatic finesse*

fir   a coniferous tree belonging to the pine family, characterized by its pyramidal style of growth, flat needles, and erect cones

fur   the fine, soft, thick, hairy coat of the skin of a mammal

fiscal   pertaining to the public treasury or revenues: *fiscal policies*; pertaining to financial matters in general: *Our fiscal year is from July 1 to June 30.*

physical   pertaining to the body: *a physical illness*; that which is material: *the physical sciences*; carnal; sexual: *a physical attraction*

flagrant   obvious; glaring: *flagrant error*; disgraceful, egregious; notorious: *a flagrant drug dealer*

fragrant   having a pleasing aroma; perfumed, aromatic: *fragrant flowers*

flair   skill; aptitude; a natural talent or ability; bent; knack: *a flair for writing comedy.*

flare   a bright light: *in case of emergency, light a flare*; an outburst; to burst out in sudden, fierce activity and passion: *Violence flared up in the ghetto after the verdict.*

flamenco   a style of dancing; a style of vocal or instrumental music originating in southern Spain

flamingo   aquatic bird with long legs and neck, webbed feet, and pinkish to scarlet plumage

flammable   combustible (technical use, on a warning sign: *caution! flammable*)

inflammable   combustible (figuratively: *inflammable emotions*)

nonflammable   not combustible or easily set on fire

flaunt   show off; display ostentatiously: *She flaunted the large diamond in her engagement ring.*

flout   show contempt for; scoff at: *He flouted convention by wearing shorts to the black tie affair.*

flea   any of numerous small, wingless bloodsucking parasitic insects that prey on mammals and birds

flee   vanish; evade, escape, avoid, shun, elude; to run away from: *If they are not watched carefully they will flee.*

flew   past tense of fly: *The birds flew south for the winter.*

flu   influenza; an acute, commonly epidemic disease characterized by respiratory symptoms and general prostration: *The child has the flu.*

flue   conduit for smoke, as in a fireplace: *Be sure to open the flue before lighting the fire.*

floe   a sheet of floating ice, as on the surface of the sea

flow   to move along in a stream; to circulate; to issue or proceed from a source

florescence   act, state, or period of flowering; bloom

fluorescence   the emission of radiation during exposure to light or X rays

flounder   to struggle clumsily: *He floundered helplessly on the first day of his new job.*; falter; waver; flop about; a marine flatfish

founder   to fall or sink down; to become wrecked; to stumble; collapse; succumb: *The project foundered because public support was lacking.*

flour   ground meal

flower   a blossom; a plant that blooms

foggy   indistinct; bewildered; blurred as if by fog; not clear; vague: *I haven't the foggiest notion of what she meant.*; thick with or having much fog; misty: *a foggy day in London town.*

fogy   a stodgy, old-fashioned, or excessively conservative person, esp. one who is intellectually dull: *She was just an old fogy who wouldn't let her granddaughter wear an earring in her nose.*

for   on behalf of; in favor of; because; since

fore   forward; front part; warning by golfer

four   a numeral

forbear   refrain or abstain from; to forgo: *I'll forbear the dessert, thank you.*

forebear   ancestor; forefather; progenitor: *My forbears came over on the Mayflower.*

forbidding   prohibiting: *They are forbidding entry.*

foreboding   a prediction; a portent of future misfortune; presentiment: *She had a foreboding that there would be an accident.*

forceful   powerful; vigorous; cogent; telling; effective: *a forceful plea for justice*

forcible   done by force: *forcible entry*

forego   go before; to precede: *forego one's partner in death*

forgo   to abstain or refrain from; do without; give up; renounce; forbear; sacrifice: *I'll forgo my dinner so that the poor child can eat.*

foreword   a short introductory statement in a published work, as a book: *A foreword is not generally written by the author of the book.*

forward   toward or at a place, point, or time in advance; onward: *a forward motion*

formally   properly; in a conventional way: *We were formally introduced.*

formerly   happening earlier in time: *We were formerly married to each other.*

fort   a fortified place occupied by troops; an army post: *The fort was well guarded.*

forte   (pronounced *fōrt*) an activity one excels in; talent, skill, knack: *The painting of landscapes is his forte.*; (pronounced *for'tay*) a direction in music to play loud and with force (opposed to *piano*, meaning soft; subdued)

forth   forward, as in *back and forth*; outward; onward: *go forth and multiply*

fourth   next after the third: *her fourth helping of dessert*

fortuitous   happening by accident or chance: *A fortuitous meeting led eventually to marriage.*

fortunate   bringing something good and unforeseen; lucky; providential: *A fortunate turn of events helped her find a new career.*

foul   unfair; unclean; rotten; grossly offensive to the senses; disgustingly loathsome: *a foul smell*; unfavorable: *foul weather*

fowl   a bird used for food or hunted as game; chicken, turkey, duck, pheasant

fraction   a number usually expressed as *1/2, 1/4, etc.*; a part as distinct from the whole of anything; portion or section: *He received only a fraction of what he was owed.*

friction   surface resistance to relative motion; the rubbing of one surface against another; discord, dissidence, antagonism, clash, contention: *The disagreement caused a lot of friction between the friends.*

frees   allows; lets loose: *He frees the animal from the trap.*
freeze   to chill, congeal, or become ice: *freeze the leftovers*
frieze   an ornamental strip: *The frieze on the antique chair was beautiful.*

friar   member of a Roman Catholic order
fryer   a small chicken suitable for frying

funeral   ceremonies for a dead person: *She cried at the funeral.*
funereal   mournful; gloomy; dismal: *She exhibited a funereal aloofness that was quite chilling.*

G

---

gaff   a metal hook fastened to a pole; to cheat; fleece; harsh treatment or criticism: *All the gaff he had to take made him even more reclusive.*
gaffe   a social blunder; faux pas: *His sudden outburst of anger was an unfortunate gaffe.*

gage   a security or a pledge; something, as a glove, thrown down as a challenge to fight: *The knight threw down his gage.*; a variety of plum, as a greengage
gauge   a measuring device; to test; a size: *twelve-gauge shotguns*; the fineness of knitted fabric: *sixty-gauge stockings*
gouge   a chisel with a rounded blade; a digging or scooping action: *to gouge a channel; to gouge holes*

gamble   to bet; to take a chance on; venture; hazard; speculation; flyer: *I'll take a gamble on the chance that I'll win.*
gambol   to skip about as in dancing or playing; frolic; spring; caper; frisk: *We love to see the deer gambol in the forest.*

gantlet a railroad track construction used in narrow places; an ordeal

gauntlet a glove; a challenge: *take up the gauntlet*

gait manner of walking, stepping, or running; the ways a horse moves: *The horse has a smooth gait.*

gate movable barrier; an opening permitting passage: *You may buy your ticket at the gate.*

garret a small attic

garrote a device or instrument used to strangle a person; strangulation or throttling

gelding a castrated male animal; a eunuch

gilding the application of gold leaf; something used to create a deceptively alluring aspect

genius exceptional natural ability; a person of extraordinarily high intelligence; gift, talent, aptitude, faculty

genus a kind; sort; class or group of individuals or of species of individuals

genteel belonging to polite society; well-bred or refined; polite; elegant: *She has the genteel demeanor of a woman of breeding.*

gentile pertaining to non-Jewish people, especially a Christian

gesture a movement of the hand, arm, body, head, or face that expresses a thought, opinion, or emotion: *a threatening gesture*; any action or communication used to express an idea or feeling: *a loving gesture*

jester one who makes jokes and funny moves; a professional clown: *the court jester*

ghastly   dreadful; horrible: *a ghastly murder*; deathlike, pallid, cadaverous

ghostly   characteristic of a ghost; phantasmal; spectral; wraithlike; unearthly: *a ghostly silence*

gibe   jeer; taunt; deride: *They gibe him whenever he tries to speak.*

jibe   shift sails; be in agreement: *Her explanation is likely to jibe with what he said.*

jive   early jazz; *Slang.* meaningless talk; to tease, fool, kid: *Don't jive me with your sweet talk.*

gild   embellish with gold: *gild the lily*

guild   organization of people with related interests: *The Writers Guild*

gilt   gold in color; golden: *gilt-edged glasses*

guilt   criminality; culpability; a crime: *His guilt was visible on his face.*

glacier   a mass of slowly moving land ice formed by the accumulation of snow on high ground

glazier   a person who fits windows with glass or panes of glass

gored   pierced with a horn:
  The bullfighter was gored; a triangular piece of material: *a gored skirt*

gourd   hard-shelled fruit of a plant: *The colorful bowls were made of gourds.*

gorilla   an ape: *It was the second time the gorilla escaped from the zoo.*

guerrilla   a member of an irregular military force: *They used guerrilla tactics to overthrow the city.*

gourmand   a person who likes food and tends to eat to excess: *He's nothing more than a gourmand who eats everything in sight.*

gourmet   connoisseur of fine food and drink: *His choice of wines shows that he is a gourmet.*

grate frame of metal bars; irritate; vex; irk; to have an irritating effect: *His constant complaining grates on my nerves.*

great immense; notable; momentous; exalted; grand: *a great performance*

gravely extremely seriously: *gravely ill*; dangerously, harmfully

gravelly covered with gravel; with a harsh, rasping sound: *His gravelly voice was a result of years of heavy smoking.*

greave a piece of plate armor for the leg between the knee and the ankle

grieve to feel great sorrow: *They grieve for the loss of their leader*; lament, weep, bewail, bemoan

grill gridiron; barbecue; interrogate: *The detective will grill him for hours to get to the facts.*

grille a metal framework; perforated screen: *The entrance had a decorative iron grille.*

grisly causing a shudder or feeling of horror; gruesome; grim: *the grisly scene of a murder*

grizzly grayish or flecked with gray; a species of bear

groan a deep, mournful sound of pain or grief: *the groans of a woman in labor*; a grating or creaking sound due to burdening with a great weight: *the groan of a heavy-laden ship navigating a turbulent ocean*

grown advanced in growth: *a grown boy*; arrived at full growth or maturity; produced or cultivated in a certain way or place: *The corn was grown in Kansas.*

guarantee a promise or assurance of quality or durability: *It has a one-year guarantee that covers parts and labor.*

guaranty a warrant; pledge; something taken as security: *He left his gold watch as a guaranty that he would bring the car back.*

guessed   arrived at an opinion without sufficient evidence to support it; estimated: *He guessed that it would take two hours to get there.*; thought: *I guessed it would be okay.*; believed: *I guessed he was telling the truth.*

guest   a person who spends time in another's home as a visitor: *house guest, dinner guest*; a person who patronizes a hotel, restaurant, etc.; participating or performing as a guest: *guest speaker, guest conductor*

H

---

hail   cheer, salute, acclaim: *hail, Caesar*; attract: *hail a cab*; precipitation in the form of ice balls

hale   healthy; robust; vigorous; sound: *The old man is still hale and hearty.*

hair   filament that grows from the skin: *Her hair was long and shiny.*

hare   rodent-like mammal having long ears; a rabbit: *The race was like the tortoise and the hare.*

hall   corridor in a building; lobby; auditorium: *The performance is in the music hall.*

haul   to pull or draw with force; drag; carry: *We have to haul away the trash.*

hallowed   sanctified; consecrated; greatly venerated: *This cemetery is hallowed ground.*

hollowed   made concave; scooped out: *A portion of the tree limb was hollowed out to make a bowl.*

halve   divide into two equal parts; to share equally; to reduce to half: *You must halve that and share it with your sister.*

have   to hold for use, contain; possess, own: *We have a new car.*

handicap   hinder, impede, incapacitate; to place at a disadvantage: *His handicap was being born into poverty.*

handicraft   a work that requires both manual and artistic skill

handiwork   work done by hand

handmade   crafted by hand rather than by machine: *handmade candles*

handmaid   a female helper or servant; something that is subservient or subordinate to another: *All good moral philosophy is but a handmaid to religion.*

homemade   made or prepared at home or in the facility or restaurant that serves it: *homemade curtains*

handsome   pleasing and dignified: *a handsome gentleman*; bounteous, liberal: *a handsome reward*

hansom   a two-wheeled covered carriage with the driver's seat at the back: *We went for a ride through Central Park in a hansom cab.*

hangar   a shed for airplanes: *The plane taxied to the hangar.*

hanger   a frame for hanging clothes: *Here is a hanger for your coat.*

hanged   executed by suspending by the neck: *He was hanged at dawn.*

hung   fastened from above with no support from below; suspended: *She hung up her clothes.*

hardy   vigorous; robust; stout; brave: *The early settlers were hardy people.*

hearty   warm-hearted; jovial; substantial: *He gave me a hearty handshake.*

heal   cure; soothe; disinfect; restore: *It's just a small cut that will heal quickly.*

heel   back part of the foot or footwear: *The shoe fits perfectly everywhere except at the heel.*

he'll   contraction for *he will*

healthful   conducive to health; wholesome: *We serve only healthful food.*

healthy   enjoying good health; hearty; robust: *The children are all healthy.*

hear   perceive by the ear; listen to; pay attention to: *I hear you.*

here   in this place: *Bring your chair over here by me.*

heard   past tense of hear; listened to: *I heard the news today.*

herd   drove or flock of animals; guard or protect: *The shepherd will herd the sheep.*

helpmate   companion and helper; husband or wife; anything that assists

helpmeet   a helpmate; spouse

[*Helpmeet* was derived from a misreading in the King James Bible where God promises Adam "to make a help meet for him," meaning a help suitable for him. As Eve became the "help," "help meet" was interpreted as "spouse."]

heroin   highly addictive narcotic derived from morphine: *He had a hard time kicking heroin.*

heroine   courageous woman; principle female character: *The heroine of the play was a great actress.*

hew   strike forcefully with a cutting instrument; to fell; to uphold or conform to rules: *hew to the tenets of the church*

hue   gradation of a color; tint: *It had a pinkish hue.*; outcry: *the hue and clamor of the crowd*

hide   conceal; cache; stash: *Hide the money under the mattress.*; the skin of an animal

hied   hurried; went quickly; hastened: *He hied himself down to the stadium.*

higher   above, taller: *That mountain is higher than the others.*; a greater amount: *Prices are higher in the city than in the country.*

hire   employ: *The company will hire another employee to complete the job.*

hoard   a stash; to store away: *In wartime people have a tendency to hoard supplies.*

horde   a wandering group or a swarm: *A horde of mosquitoes invaded the camp.*

hoarse   harsh; grating; throaty; rough: *His voice was hoarse from screaming at the game.*

horse   large, four-legged animal: *She rode the horse into the woods.*

hole   an opening in something or an unoccupied space; a playing period in golf: *We only had time to play nine holes.*; a lack or a fault: *Your reasoning is full of holes.*

whole   a single entity comprised of a collection of parts; including all of an entity: *This requires your whole attention.*

holy   sacred; hallowed: *holy ground*

holey   full of holes: *holey cheese*

wholly   completely; entirely: *The group was wholly in favor of the proposition.*

home   one's own house or residence; abode, dwelling, habitation; domicile; asylum: *Home is where the heart is.*

hone   a whetstone for sharpening cutting tools; to make more acute or effective; perfect: *He honed his skills at his father's side.*

homely   plain; unattractive: *a homely mongrel*; lacking refinement: *a homely country boy*

homey   comfortably informal; cozy; homelike; warm and friendly: *a homey cottage*

homogeneous   of the same kind or nature; unvarying; unmixed: *a homogeneous population*

homogenous   alike in structure because of a common origin: *a homogenous breed*

homogonous   pertaining to flowers that do not differ in the relative length of stamens and pistils (opposed to *heterogonous*)

homographs   words that are spelled identically but may   or may not share a pronunciation, such as *sow* (sō) meaning *to scatter seed*, and *sow* (sou) meaning *an adult female swine*

homonym   a word the same as another in sound and spelling but different in meaning such as *light*, meaning either *illumination* or *of little weight*

homophones   words that sound alike whether or not they are spelled differently: *holy* and *wholly*

hoop   a circular band of metal, wood, or other stiff material; the metal ring from which a basketball net is suspended; rim

whoop   a loud cry or shout, as of excitement or joy; to cry as an owl or a crane

hostel   an inexpensive lodging place for young people; an inn: *The students stayed at a youth hostel.*

hostile   warlike, aggressive:
a hostile takeover; adverse, contrary, unsympathetic: *a hostile response*

hour   a measurement of time: *I'll be ready in an hour.*

our   belonging to us; possessive of we: *We have our new home.*

how ever   when "ever" is used for emphasis: *How ever did you do that?*

however   by whatever means; to whatever degree; nevertheless: *It had started to rain; however, the ball game continued.*

human   pertaining to or having the nature of people: *It's only human to want to be in love.*

humane   merciful; kind; tender; compassionate: *Children and animals should always have humane treatment.*

humerus   long bone of the upper arm: *She broke her humerus.*

humorous   marked by humor; funny, witty: *She always says something humorous.*

hurdle   a barrier; problem; obstacle: *He jumped over the last hurdle.*

hurtle   speed; race; rush; shoot: *I watched the horses hurtle down the track.*

hyperbola   a plane curve having two branches
hyperbole   an exaggeration used as a figure of speech: *That dog's so ugly its face could stop a clock.*

hypercritical   excessively critical: *He is hypercritical with his students.*
hypocritical   falsely claiming feelings; being deceptive: *I do not appreciate your hypocritical praise.*

I

---

idle   not in use; unemployed; inactive: *The lifeguard was idle during the winter months.*
idol   object of worship; a person blindly adored: *The rock star was an idol to many teenagers.*
idyll   narrative poem; carefree experience: *Their affair was simply a romantic idyll.*

illegal   forbidden by law or statute: *an illegal U-turn*; forbidden by official rules or regulations: *an illegal block* (in football); something that is unacceptable to or not performed by a computer: *an illegal operation*
illegitimate   born out of wedlock: *an illegitimate child*; not sanctioned by law or custom: *an illegitimate action*; not in proper grammatical usage
illicit   not legally permitted or authorized: *an illicit attempt to control the market*; unlicensed; prohibited; not permitted by custom; disapproved of or not permitted for moral or ethical reasons
unlawful   contrary to law: *unlawful search and seizure*; born out of wedlock

[All of the above describe actions that are not in accord with the law. However, there are some differences in meaning among the words. *Illegal* refers most specifically to violations of statutes or codified rules: *illegal seizure of property*. *Illegitimate* means lacking legal or traditional rights:

illegitimate use of privileged information. Illicit most often applies to matters regulated by law with emphasis on the way things are carried out: *illicit conversion of property. Unlawful* means not sanctioned by law: *an unlawful claim to an inheritance.*]

illegible   impossible or hard to read: *The handwriting was illegible.*
unreadable   not interesting; not worth reading: *The book was unreadable.*

immunity   being unaffected by something; a resistance to disease: *The vaccine gave the children immunity to polio.*; a legally established condition: *The court granted the witness immunity from prosecution.*
impunity   exemption from punishment or harm: *He carried out his evil act with impunity.*

impassable   impossible to travel over or across: *The swollen river was impassable.*
impassible   incapable of feeling pain; incapable of emotion: *He seemed impassible in spite of the severity of his injuries.*

imperial   relating to an empire, emperor, or empress: *an imperial ruler;* regal; outstanding in quality
imperious   tyrannical; despotic; arrogant; dictatorial; overbearing: *behaving in an imperious way;* urgent; imperative: *an imperious requirement*
imperil   risk, jeopardize, hazard, chance; to put in peril or danger: *imperil the safe outcome of an action*

imply   signify or mean; to suggest: *Her words imply a lack of caring.*
infer   deduce, reason, guess; draw a conclusion: *They inferred her dislike from her cold reply.*

imposter   charlatan, fake, fraud, pretender: *He claimed to be a prince, but he was only an imposter.*
imposture   the act of deceiving by assuming a false identity; fraud, hoax, swindle

impugn   to attack as untrue; censure; malign; to cast doubt upon: *Her reputation was impugned.*

impute   to attribute or ascribe something discreditable: *He imputed the error to the salesperson.*

in   inclusion within a space: *He ran in the park. The pie is in the oven.*

into   to the inside of: *She came into the building.*; in toward: *I'm going into town.*

inane   empty, pointless, lacking sense, complacently foolish: *I was bored by the lecturer's inane presentation.*

insane   afflicted with mental derangement, having a disordered mind, mad: *Her bizarre threats were the result of an insane jealousy.*

inapt   unsuited; incapable; clumsy; inappropriate: *His inapt response did not address the issue.*

inept   bungling; stupid; inane; foolish; unskillful: *His inept handling of the ball cost them the game.*

incidence   the rate or range of occurrence or influence of something: *There is a high incidence of lung cancer in people who smoke.*

incidents   individual events; a distinct bit of action; occurrences: *There were several disturbing incidents during the peace march.*

incinerate   burn up, reduce to ashes: *incinerate the evidence*

insinuate   hint, suggest, imply, introduce artfully: *Did you mean to insinuate that I am wrong?*

incipient   beginning to exist; developing: *It was more than friendship; it was an incipient romance.*

insipient   unwise; foolish: *Their office flirtation soon turned into an insipient affair.*

incite   instigate; induce; arouse; goad; provoke: *incite a riot*

insight   perception; intuition; understanding: *The older we get, the more insight we acquire.*

incredible   unbelievable; not convincing: *His story is incredible.*

incredulous   skeptical; disinclined to believe: *I'm incredulous of his alibi.*

incubate   to hatch eggs by sitting on them or by artificial heat; to develop, grow, take form: *Her plan would slowly incubate in her mind.*

intubate   to insert a tube into the larynx or the like, as in a medical procedure: *The doctor had to intubate the patient.*

indeterminable   incapable of being ascertained, measured, or fixed; incapable of being decided: *an indeterminable conflict*

indeterminate   lacking precision or clarity; not known in advance: *an indeterminate amount of time*

interminable   boringly protracted; unending; incessant: *interminable whining*

indict   charge with an offense; criticize: *He tends to indict everyone of plotting against him.*

indite   compose or write, as a poem: *She will indite an ode to the sunset.*

indigenous   innate; inherent; natural; aboriginal: *Remarkable agility is indigenous to the tribe.*

indigent   poor; impoverished; distressed: *The indigent street people are often ignored.*

indignant   filled with anger at a person who is regarded as unjust, mean, or unworthy: *She was indignant about her coworker's accusations.*

indiscreet   lacking prudence; revealing secrets: *She made an indiscreet remark about their relationship.*

indiscrete not divided into distinct parts: *a box of indiscrete personnel files*

indolent not inclined to exert oneself, slothful; conducive to laziness, languorous
insolent abrasive; arrogant; brazenly impudent; impertinent

ineluctable not to be avoided or overcome; inescapable
unelectable not capable of, or having a reasonable chance of getting elected, as to public office

inequity unfairness; bias; favoritism: *She treated her two sons with inequity.*
iniquity wickedness; unrighteousness; evildoing, infamy, depravity; gross injustice: *I have loved justice and hated iniquity; therefore, I die in exile.*

infarction a localized area of tissue that is dying or dead, having been deprived of its blood supply because of an obstruction
infraction breach; violation; infringement: *infraction of the rules*; in medicine, an incomplete fracture of a bone

infect affect with disease; contaminate; damage
infest overrun or beset: *shark-infested waters*

inflection an alteration in pitch or tone of the voice; a change in the form of a word indicating number, person, or tense
infliction impose something painful or unwelcome upon; physical assault

ingenious characterized by cleverness or originality of invention or construction: *an ingenious device*; brilliant; resourceful
ingenuous simple; straightforward; open; naïve; artlessly frank; candid; innocent: *a con artist with the ingenuous smile of a child*

ingrate   an ungrateful person

ingratiate   bring oneself into favor: *She ingratiated herself with the children by bringing gingerbread cookies.*

inhabit   be present in, make one's home or live in: *I inhabit a remodeled church.*

inhibit   hold in check, restrain: *The police officer will inhibit rowdy behavior.*

inherent   innate; existing as a permanent, inseparable element or quality: *an inherent love for animals*

inherit   receive a right as an heir: *inherit the farm*; receive a genetic character: *inherit blue eyes*

inhuman   unfeeling, not sympathetic, savage; not suited for human beings; not human

inhumane   lacking humanity, kindness, compassion, etc.; cruel to animals; brutal

insidious   progressing inconspicuously but harmfully: *an insidious disease*; treacherous; crafty; stealthily deceitful: *an insidious agreement*; corrupting; cunning, wily

invidious   unfairly discriminating; injurious; hateful; calculated to give offense; causing animosity or resentment: *an invidious comment*

insinuate   to hint at: *She insinuated that they were having an affair.*; to instill subtly or slyly, as into the mind: *to insinuate doubts*; inject, inculcate

intimate   to indicate or make known indirectly: *She intimated that they were married.*

insolate   expose to the sun's rays

insolent   presumptuous; arrogant; impertinent: *His insolent remarks were not well received.*

insulate   protect from heat or electricity

insoluble   incapable of being dissolved; incapable of being explained
insolvable   incapable of being solved

install   invest, instate, place in position; connect for use: *install an air conditioner*; induct into office with ceremonies: *install a new president*
instill   inculcate, introduce; insinuate; infuse slowly into the mind or feelings: *instill a sense of fairness in a child*

instance   an occurrence of something; an example: *The fistfight was an instance of student discord.*
instants   very brief time periods; almost imperceptible moments: *We experience only instants of pure joy.*

instinct   innate aspect of behavior; strong impulse; natural capability or aptitude: *He acted on instinct.*
intuition   knowing without the use of natural processes; acute insight: *She had an intuition that her children were in danger.*
prescience   knowledge of things before they exist or happen; foresight: *He had a prescience that there would be an earthquake.*

intelligent   wise, shrewd, having the capacity for thought and reason: *The professor is an intelligent man.*
intelligible   well articulated or enunciated and loud enough to be heard; can be understood: *He was an intelligible speaker.*

intense   in an extreme degree; straining; profoundly earnest: *He is intense when it comes to writing his novel.*
intents   aims, purposes; intentions: *His intents are to be rich and famous.*

interment   the act or ritual of burial: *The interment will be at noon at the Midtown Cemetery.*
internment   the act of undergoing training; confinement of enemy aliens, prisoners of war, and political prisoners: *During World War II, many Japanese Americans were sent to internment camps.*

intern   apprentice; trainee: *She was an intern at the White House.*

internee   a person who has been confined, as a prisoner of war: *He was an internee of the Germans.*

internist   a physician specializing in diagnosis and treatment of diseases: *You should see an internist about the pain in your stomach.*

Internet, the   a large computer network linking smaller computer networks worldwide

intranet   a computer network with restricted access, as within a company, that uses protocols developed by the Internet

interstate   connecting different states: *interstate commerce*; a highway serving more than one state: *the U.S. Interstate Highway System*

intestate   said of a person who dies without having made a will: *No one knows who her heirs should be because she died intestate.*

intrastate   operating within the boundaries of a state: *intrastate companies*

intractable   not easily controlled; not manageable; stubborn; obstinate: *an intractable employee*

untrackable   that which cannot be traced: *an untrackable letter*

inveterate   firmly established by long continuance, as a disease; chronic; settled or confirmed in a habit, practice, or feeling: *He's an inveterate runner.*

invertebrate   without a backbone; without strength of character: *She's an invertebrate who will lie about anything to stay out of trouble.*

its   belonging to it: *This is its handle.*

it's   it is: *It's cold outside.*; it has: *It's been a long winter.*

J

jam   fill too tightly; cram; fruit preserve
jamb   vertical sides of a doorway or window

judicial   pertaining to a judge; judging; forensic
judicious   using sound judgment; practical

juggler   one who keeps several objects, such as balls or chainsaws, in continuous motion in the air by tossing and catching; one who uses trickery or deception
jugular   related to or situated in the region of the neck or throat; a vital and vulnerable trait, feature, or element that one attacks in an attempt to overcome an adversary swiftly and completely: *go for the jugular*

K

kernel   the central, softer part within a hard shell of a nut or fruit stone; the whole seed of grain such as wheat or corn: *Popcorn is made from the kernel of corn.*; the nucleus or essential part of anything: *There was a kernel of truth in everything she said.*
colonel   a commissioned officer in the armed forces

kibbutz   a community settlement organized under collectivist principles
kibitz   to offer unwanted advice or criticism; to be a busybody

knap   crest of a small hill; to strike; break off or chip
nap   to doze; fibers on the surface of cloth; a downy coating

knave   unprincipled, dishonest person; villain
nave   the center part of a church

knead   work dough or clay into a mass; massage

kneed   struck or touched with the knee
need   lack; requirement; necessity

knight   a man awarded a nonhereditary title (Sir) by a sovereign in recognition of merit; a man devoted to the service of a woman
night   darkness between sunset and sunrise

knit   to make something by interlocking loops of yarn with knitting needles; grow together, as broken bones; become intimately united: *knit a friendship*
nit   the egg of a parasitic insect, such as a louse or flea

knot   cord, rope, ribbon, or the like that is tied or folded upon itself; a tangle in hair; a difficulty: *a knotty problem*
not   expressing negation, denial, or prohibition: *I will not answer your question.*

know   to understand as true: *I know the sun will come up tomorrow.*; to be aware of: *I know his eyes are green.*; to be acquainted with: *I know her sister.*
no   a negative: *The answer is no.*; a refusal or denial: *No, I don't have it.*

noes   negative votes
nose   part of the face that contains nostrils and the organs of smell, used for breathing; prow of a ship; forward end of an aircraft; a perceptive faculty: *a nose for news*

L

label   an attachment that indicates the manufacturer, size, destination, or nature of something: *According to the label this is a "large."*; a brief description of a person or group: *Don't label me a "liberal" just because I want to protect the environment.*
labile   flexible; likely to change

lacks   does not have something that is needed: *The safe lacks a lock.*
lax   loose or slack; not firm; not strict; negligent: *lax in enforcing the rules*

lade   load; to put cargo on board a ship; to lift out of, as a fluid: *lade soup;* to burden: *laden with debt*
laid   past and past participle of *lay;* placed on a surface: *laid down his burden;* to put into a certain state: *laid carpet*

lain   past participle of *lie;* rested; reposed
lane   narrow way or passage; an ocean route

lair   a wild animal's den or resting place; a person's hiding place
layer   a thickness of matter covering a surface: *layers of clothing;* a hen that lays eggs

lam   a hasty escape; fleeing or hiding from the law: *on the lam*
lamb   a young sheep; a person who is gentle or innocent; a person who is easily cheated

lama   Tibetan or Mongolian Buddhist monk
llama   an animal with soft woolly fleece

lath   strip of wood
lathe   machine for shaping material

laps   more than one lap: *She swam five laps in the pool. My cat sits in the laps of all of my guests whether they like her or not.*
lapse   a temporary deviation; a slip or error: *a lapse of judgment;* discontinuance due to a late payment: *She let her insurance lapse.*

laud   to praise, honor, extol
loud   having great volume or intensity; *The band is very loud.;* tastelessly showy; *I would not wear such a loud shirt.*

lay   set down; place; past tense of *lie*
lei   a garland of flowers worn around the neck
lie   rest in a horizontal position; recline

leach   to dissolve out substances; to percolate
leech   bloodsucking worm; extortioner; sponger

lead   to conduct or escort: *lead them out*; a heavy bluish-gray metal
led   past tense of lead: *He led them along the path.*

leak   to allow the passage of a substance through a flaw: *There is a water leak in the pipe under the sink.*; a breach of secrecy: *They leaked the story to the press.*
leek   a plant related to the onion with a slender bulb and dark green leaves

lean   to incline: *lean on me*; thin, skinny, lank, lanky; sparse; economical
lien   legal claim

leased   rented for a specified time: *She leased a car.*
least   smallest; slightest degree: *That's the least of her concerns.*

legislator   one who makes laws: *This is his first term of office as a legislator.*
legislature   a group invested with the power to make, alter, and repeal laws: *The legislature will convene again in January.*

lend   to grant the use of something that will be returned; to make a loan: *I agreed to lend him the money.*; to help: *lend a hand*
loan   the act of lending: *the loan of a book*; money lent: *The bank granted the loan.*

[Some contend that *lend* is a verb and *loan* is a noun. However, *loan* as a verb meaning to lend has been used in English for nearly eight hundred years. *Loan* is most common in financial contexts.]

lent granted the use of something for a period of time: *lent a book*; allowed the use of money at interest

Lent the period from Ash Wednesday to Holy Saturday, devoted to fasting and penitence

lint fabric with a raised nap, used for dressing wounds; fluff; minute shreds of yarn

lessen to cause to decrease; to belittle; to become less; reduce: *The pain will lessen with time.*

lesson something to be learned; a class; a teaching: *The lesson is to look before you leap.*

lesser smaller: *She received a lesser amount.*; inferior: *a lesser evil*

lessor a person who grants a lease: *The lessor agreed to let me stay another month.*

levee embankment to prevent flooding: *The levee might fail in hurricane conditions.*

levy to impose a tax: *to levy a duty on imports*; the amount owed or collected; the conscription of troops

liable responsible: *He's liable for the damage to her car.*; likely: *She's liable to bring a date.*

libel in law, defamation by written or printed words, pictures, or in any form other than by spoken words or gestures; anything that is defamatory or that maliciously or damagingly misrepresents

liar a person who does not tell the truth; falsifier, perjurer, prevaricator: *a dirty, rotten liar*

lyre a stringed musical instrument

lightening   becoming lighter or brighter: *The sky began lightening as the storm passed.*

lightning   a brilliant electric discharge in the sky: *The dark sky was pierced by lightning.*

limb   large branch of a tree; an arm, leg, or wing

limn   to draw; portray in words; describe

limpet   any of various marine gastropod mollusks with a shallow conical shell and a broad muscular foot that sticks tightly to rocks: *stuck like limpets to the spot, lest they forgot*

limpid   clear, transparent, as water or eyes: *a limpid pool*; lucid; easily comprehended: *a limpid style of writing*

linage   the number of printed lines; the amount charged (or paid) per printed line

lineage   ancestry, pedigree, parentage, genealogy

lineal   being in the direct line, as a descendant: *lineal heir*

linear   consisting of or using lines: *linear design*

links   the rings of which a chair is composed; bonds or ties; connections

lynx   a wildcat having long limbs, a short tail, and tufted ears

liqueur   sweet alcoholic after-dinner drink

liquor   an alcoholic drink; meat or vegetable broth: *pot liquor*

litany   ceremonial form of prayer; prolonged or tedious account; list; enumeration

liturgy   a form of public worship; ritual; a particular arrangement of religious services

literal   taking words in their primary sense without metaphor or allegory:

the literal meaning of a word; expressed by letters; actual, factual, truthful, exact, reliable

littoral   pertaining to the shore of a lake, the sea, etc.; a region lying along a shore

load   a burden or cargo
lode   an ore deposit

loaner   one who loans; something loaned: *While my car's in the body shop, I'm driving a loaner.*
loner   one who prefers to be alone or is rarely in the company of others: *A loner doesn't go to many parties.*

loath   unwilling; reluctant: *She was loath to go.*
loathe   abominate; hate: *They loathe each other.*

local   pertaining to a particular place: *local custom*
locale   location; scene or setting, as in a film, play, or novel: *filmed in a desert locale*

lodge   cabin, hut, cottage, the main building of a camp or hotel
loge   the front section of the first balcony; a private box or enclosure

loose   not tight or bound: *loose clothing*
lose   to experience loss: *lose your keys; lose money*

loot   booty; spoils or plunder taken by pillaging; to ransack, plunder: *loot the art museums*
lute   a stringed musical instrument

lubricate   to make slippery or smooth; apply a lubricant to a machine to diminish friction; to smooth over a problem; ease: *to lubricate a family squabble*

lucubrate   to write in a scholarly way; to work, write, or study laboriously, especially late at night: *She would be a more well-rounded person if she didn't lucubrate so much.*

lucent   shining; luminous; translucent: *softly lucent as a rounded moon*

lucid   easily understood; comprehensible; rational or sane: *He's a muddled fool, full of lucid intervals.*

lumbar   relating to the loin, especially the lower back area: *a pain in the lumbar region*

lumber   logs or timber cut for use; to move in a slow, clumsy, noisy way: *He lumbers along like an old, angry bear.*

luxuriant   lush; rich in growth, teeming, fruitful, prolific, copious, abundant: *a luxuriant crop of sunflowers*

luxuriate   greatly enjoy oneself; revel: *to luxuriate in wealth*; thrive: *The roses luxuriate in the sunny garden.*

luxurious   rich, sumptuous; promoting luxury: *The hotel room was luxurious.*

M

maddening   driving to madness or frenzy; exasperating: *All those delays are maddening.*

madding   frenzied; raging: *far from the madding crowd*

made   past tense of *make*; prepared: *made dinner*; contrived: *made a false statement*

maid   female servant: *The maid cleaned our room.*; a girl or young unmarried woman: *a fair maid*

magnate   a person of great influence, importance, or standing in a particular enterprise: *a hotel magnate*; a person of distinction: *a literary magnate*

magnet a thing or person that attracts: *The race track is a magnet for compulsive gamblers.*; a thing that has the property of attracting certain substances, such as iron or stainless steel: *She puts notes on the refrigerator with a magnet.*; a lodestone

mail the letters and packages that are transported by the postal service; to send via the postal service: *I will mail the letter for you.*; flexible armor made of interlinked metal rings: *The knight wore mail into battle.*

male being of the human or animal sex which begets offspring; the sex that produces gametes (spermatozoa)

main chief: *the main person in charge*; principal: *main reason*

mane neck hair of an animal; a person's long hair: *a luxurious mane*

maize a pale yellow resembling the color of corn: *She wore a lovely maize dress.*

maze labyrinth; any complex system that causes confusion: *a maze of government regulations*; a state of bewilderment: *The crowded street was a maze of pushing and screaming people.*

malady illness; affliction; complaint: *He had a chronic malady that sapped all of his energy.*; any undesirable or disordered condition: *a social malady*

melody musical sounds; harmony; tune; song

mall a large retail complex; area used as a public walk

maul a heavy hammer; to use roughly; to injure

moll a female criminal

manner way of doing something; behavior

manor a landed estate; mansion

mantel   facing of a fireplace; a shelf above: *Put the clock on the mantel.*

mantle   a cloak; something that conceals: *the mantle of darkness*

marry   take a husband or wife; wed; combine, connect, join: *The new cars marry fuel efficiency and roominess.*

merry   happy, cheery, glad; jolly, jovial, mirthful; joyous in disposition: *a merry old elf*

marshal   high-ranking military officer; to arrange in order; convoke; gather: *marshal the forces*

martial   warlike; associated with armed forces: *martial law*

marten   a carnivore of the genus *Martes* of northern wooded areas

martin   a bird that resembles and is closely related to the swallow

massage   a treatment consisting of rubbing and kneading the body to increase suppleness and relieve tension; to manipulate data to produce a desired result: *massage the figures*

message   a communication sent by mail, e-mail, messenger, telephone, etc.; an official communication; a prophetic pronouncement: *That cough is a message that your cold is getting worse.*

massed   gathered, assembled: *The stores were massed in the downtown area.*

mast   a structure rising above the hull of a boat or ship to hold sails; any upright pole, such as a mast for a flag: *The flag was flown at half mast.*

masterful   dominating; self-willed: *The envoy's masterful behavior irritated the citizens.*

masterly   like or befitting a master: *a masterly presentation of his paintings*

mat   a flat piece of material used to place under an object, such as a dish; a floor pad: *a doormat*

matte   a dull finish, as on glass, metal, or paper: *a glossy or matte photo*

material   substance out of which a thing can be made: *I bought the material for the drapes.*

materiel   equipment and supplies of a military force; an aggregate of things used in any business or undertaking: *requisition the necessary materiel for the operation*

mean   intend: *What do you mean?*; signify, indicate, imply; malicious: *a mean bully*

mien   a person's look or bearing: *a woman of regal mien*

meat   food; the flesh of animals; edible part of anything: *the meat of a walnut*; the essential part: *the meat of the matter*

meet   join: *the roads meet here*; become acquainted with: *I'd like you to meet my friend.*

mete   deal; measure; dole: *to mete out punishment*

meatier   having more meat; more thought-provoking: *a meatier subject*

meteor   a fiery streak in the sky produced by a meteoroid passing through the earth's atmosphere; a shooting star; something or someone that moves with spectacular speed: *a meteoric rise in popularity*

medal   a metal decoration; a reward: *She received a medal for her bravery.*

meddle   intervene; intrude; pry: *Don't meddle in other people's business.*

median   relating to the middle: *a median strip in a highway*; a midpoint, line, or plane: *The median cost of a home is higher than ever.*

medium   about halfway between extremes: *The shirt was a size medium.*; an agency by which something is conveyed: *the medium of television*

meretricious   showy; gaudy; tawdry; based on pretense; false: *a meretricious comment*

meritorious   deserving of praise, admirable: *meritorious service*

metal   a hard substance such as gold, silver, or copper
mettle   inherent quality of character; fortitude; courage

mewl   to cry or whimper as an infant or young child: *the infant, mewling and puking in the nurse's arms*
mule   the offspring of a female horse and a male donkey; a stubborn person; a lounging slipper

mews   soft, high-pitched sounds of cats or kittens; characteristic sounds gulls make
muse   think, ruminate on, dream, ponder, contemplate: *I mused on his offer for a long time.*

midst   core, heart; occurring in the middle: *She arrived at the theater in the midst of the performance.*; course of action
missed   failed to hit: *missed the target*; regretted the loss or absence of: *She missed her classmates.*; failed to be present: *missed church*
mist   cloud; a fine spray; to rain in very fine drops; something that dims or obscures: *The mist of passion blurred his reason.*

might   force; strength; past tense of *may*
mite   tiny particle; an insect; a small amount

mince   cut into very small pieces: *mince onions*; soften or moderate one's words: *mince words*; to walk with short dainty steps: *She minces along like a little girl.*
mints   plural of *mint*; aromatic herbs; candies; produces money: *mints coins*

mind   that which reasons, thinks, feels, wills, perceives, etc.; intellect or understanding; to care: *Do you mind if I smoke?*; to tend: *mind the baby*; heed or obey: *mind the teacher*
mined   dug into the earth to extract ore, coal, precious stones, etc.; drew useful information from: *He mined all of the reports on the subject.*

miner   a person who works in a mine; a mechanical device used in mining

minor   underage person

minks   weasel-like animals; fur coats made of this animal: *He gives her minks and diamonds.*

minx   an impudent or flirtatious girl: *The minx likes his expensive presents.*

miserly   like a miser; cheap, stingy, penurious: *He is not miserly with his gifts.*

misery   tribulation, suffering; grief, anguish, torment, desolation: *the misery of abject poverty*

missal   a book of prayers or devotions

missile   an object or weapon for throwing or shooting

misses   plural of miss (a title of respect for an unmarried woman); sizes of women's garments

missis   wife; the mistress of a household

moan   a prolonged low sound as from pain of some sort; a lamentation; groan; grieve; mourn

mown   past participle of *mow: He has mown the grass.*

modal   pertaining to mode, manner, or form; in music, based on a scale other than major or minor

model   a standard or example for imitation; exemplary: *a model prisoner;* a miniature representation of something: *a model train;* a person or thing that serves as a subject for an artist

module   a separable component or self-contained segment of something else: *an office module;* a standard unit for measuring; in computers, a program or part that performs a distinct function

mode   method, manner; a way: *a new mode of travel*

mowed   past tense of mow: *He mowed the lawn.*

Monseigneur   a French title of honor or respect given to princes and prelates

Monsignor   a prelate with a rank or title that is usually conferred by the Pope

mood   a frame of mind; temper, humor, disposition, inclination: *She's not in the mood to go to a party.*; a prevailing attitude: *the mood of the voters*

mooed   past tense of *moo*, the sound a cow makes

moor   a tract of peaty wasteland with poor drainage; to secure a vehicle such as a boat, ship, or dirigible in a particular place; to fix firmly; secure: *moor the ship to the dock*

Moor   a Muslim of the mixed Berber and Arab people inhabiting northwest Africa

more   in greater quantity, amount, measure, degree, or number: *I need more time.*

moot   debatable; undecided: *a moot point*; disputable, unsettled

mute   silent; refraining from speech; incapable of speech; to deaden or muffle the sound of

moral   ethical: *moral responsibility*; lesson: *the moral of a story*; upright, honest, straightforward, virtuous, honorable: *a moral woman*

morale   spirit; mood; emotional or mental condition: *the morale of the soldiers*

morality   character or virtue; concern with the distinction between good and evil or right conduct; the right principles of human conduct: *morality lessons*

mortality   the quality or state of being mortal; death rate; the ratio of deaths in a given area to the population of that area: *mortality figures*

morays tropical eels having porelike gill openings and no pectoral fins: *moray eel*

mores (pronounced *moray*) customs, conventions, practices: *The settlers brought the mores of the old country with them.*

morning early day: *We leave early tomorrow morning.*

mourning sorrowing or lamentation: *She couldn't stop mourning the loss of her dog.*

motif recurring theme, subject, or idea: *the motif of the song*

motive motivation; ground; cause; reason: *Her motive was questionable.*

mouse a small rodent; a computer device

mousse a dessert made with whipped cream; a gel or foam used to keep the hair in place

moose a large mammal of the deer family; a member of a fraternal association

muscle brawn; power; force; organ that produces movement

mussel a bivalve mollusk or clam

musical pertaining to music: *a musical instrument*; tuneful; melodious; harmonious; dulcet; lyrical

musicale a music program forming the main part of a social occasion

Muslim a believer in Islam; also Moslem

muslin sturdy cotton fabric

mussed messy; untidy; tangled: *mussed hair*

must ought; should; obliged, bound, required, or compelled to: *You must be on time.*; a necessity; vital: *A warm coat is a must in this weather.*

mustard   a pungent powder of the mustard plant, used for seasoning food

mustered   convoked; gathered; convened; congregated: *They mustered the troops.*

mystic   pertaining to esoteric, otherworldly, or occult practices; a person who claims to have insight into mysteries not understood by ordinary people

mystique   someone or something that has an aura of mystery or mystical power

---

N

---

naval   of the navy: *Naval Academy*; pertaining to ships: *naval battle*

navel   the depression in the center of the belly where the umbilical cord had been attached

nay   refusal; denial; negative vote

neigh   high-pitched sound made by a horse

noisome   offensive or disgusting, as an odor; harmful; noxious; stinking: *noisome factory emissions*

noisy   loud, harsh, or confused sounds; clamorous; tumultuous; vociferous: *noisy football fans.*

no body   no group: *There is no body of literature on the topic.*; no deceased person: *We believed he was dead but no body was ever found*

nobody   no person: *Nobody left the house during the storm. Nobody is home.*

no one   nobody: *No one understands the problem.*

none   not one; not any: *None of them attended the event.*; nothing: *She looked for a reason but found none.*; to no extent; no way

nun   a woman of a religious order: *My teacher in Catholic school was a nun.*

notable   prominent, important, or distinguished; famous; great; eminent: *a notable philanthropist*

noted   well-known; celebrated: *a noted musician*

notorious   widely and unfavorably known; disreputable; infamous: *a notorious bank robber*

numerable   capable of being counted, totaled, or numbered: *numerable reasons*

numerous   very many; existing in great quantity: *Numerous people crowded the stadium.*

O

---

oar   a long pole used to row a boat

o'er   over

ore   a mineral from which a metal can be extracted for profit

ode   a lyric poem expressive of exalted or enthusiastic emotion

owed   obliged to pay; indebted: *He still owed money on his car loan.*; to have a feeling toward someone or something: *He owed me gratitude for my help.*

odious   arousing hatred; abhorrent; repugnant; abominable; loathsome, detestable: *an odious pedophile*

odorous   having a distinctive odor; smelly: *an odorous stockyard*

official   authorized, authoritative: *We obtained official permission to enter the building.*; one who administers the rules of a game: *The official called for a time-out.*

officious   meddlesome; intrusive in an offensive manner: *She's an officious woman who makes a nuisance of herself.*

oleo   margarine: *I prefer butter to oleo.*

olio   a dish of many ingredients; hodgepodge; medley or potpourri; miscellany: *an olio of gadgets*

one   a single unit, object, or being

won   past tense of win; basic unit of money in North and South Korea

on to   go forward: *moved on to the next phase*

onto   to place or position upon: *He put his glasses onto the table.*; to be aware of: *I'm onto your wily ways.*

ophthalmologist   physician specializing in the eye

optician   one who makes lenses and eyeglasses

optometrist   one who examines eyes and measures vision

oral   spoken rather than written: *oral exam*; relating to the mouth: *oral cavity*

verbal   relating to words: *verbal ability*; using words alone without action: *verbal imagery*; literal: *a verbal translation*

ordinance   law, practice, or custom; religious rite

ordnance   military weapons as a whole; heavy guns; artillery

orient   to place so as to face the east; to become familiar with a situation

Orient   the countries of Asia (The Orient)

overdo   to do to excess: *overdo exercise*; to take to extremes; to cook too long: *overdo the steak*

overdue   past due; deserved but not yet to come: *Your reward is far overdue.*

overseas   abroad; across the sea: *overseas travel*; beyond the sea; foreign: *overseas assignment*

oversees   supervises: *oversees the manufacturing division*; manages; surveys, as from a higher point; looks over; examines: *oversees the documents*

P

paced   walked briskly; stepped; trotted; ran; trudged: *The father-to-be paced up and down.*

paste   fasten or stick: *Paste the paper to the wall.*; a creamy topping: *almond paste*; any soft, smooth, and plastic material or preparation; an artificial gem: *That's not a diamond but only paste.*

pack   small package of similar items: *a pack of tissues*; bundle; a group of people, animals, or things: *pack of wolves*

pact   formal agreement; treaty: *a pact with Germany*

pail   a cylindrical vessel with a handle; a bucket: *Fetch a pail of water.*

pale   pallid; light; feeble; weak: *The patient looked pale and thin.*

pain   to feel hurt; suffering; misery; torment; ache, agony, anguish

pane   a glass-filled section of a window or door

pang   a sudden sharp feeling of distress or longing: *a pang of desire*; *a pang of guilt*; twinge, ache, throb, stab

pair   two things that are matched for use together: *a pair of socks*; a married, engaged, or dating couple; two mated animals; *a pair of horses*

pare   to cut off the outer coating, layer, or part of: *pare an apple*

pear   an edible fruit; the tree itself: *partridge in a pear tree*

palate   the roof of the mouth; taste: *a fine palate for gourmet food*

palette   an artist's paint board; the set of colors on such a board

pallet   bed; platform; a shaping tool used by potters

paltry   trashy, worthless: *The prize was too paltry to justify an effort to win.*; contemptible: *The paltry wage that they offer is an insult.*

poultry   chickens, turkeys, ducks, and geese raised for food

parameter   a measurable characteristic; a constant factor serving as a limit; guidelines: *the basic parameters of our foreign policy*

perimeter   the circumference or outline of a closed figure; outer boundary of an enclosed area: *the perimeter of the estate*

parish   an ecclesiastical district, a church with its field of activity

perish   expire, shrivel, wither, rot, vanish

partition   distribution in portions or shares; apportion; a separation: *a partition between offices*; a part, division, or section

petition   a formally drawn request: *a petition for clemency*; to beg for or request something; solicitation, appeal; suit: *petition the court*

passed   gone beyond; happened: *and so it passed*; moved on; died: *The old man has passed on.*

past   no longer current: *the account is past due*; formerly: *a past president*

patience   capacity of calm endurance; forbearance: *She has the patience of a saint.*

patients   those under medical treatment: *The patients are responding to treatment.*

pause   suspension; interruption; a temporary stop: *Put the tape on pause.*; a momentary hesitation: *He paused frequently during his speech to wait for the applause.*

paws   the feet of animals; to scrape with paws: *The dog always paws the door to get in.*

peace   quiet, calm, rapport, concord, truce; lack of hostility: *a time of peace*

piece   part; section; fragment; portion: *a piece of cake*; a musical or literary composition

peak   pinnacle; acme; zenith: *a mountain peak*

peek   to look or glance quickly or furtively: *peek at the presents*

pique   offend; excite: *Her curiosity was piqued.*

peal   a ringing of a set of bells; chime: *The church bells peal Christmas carols.*
peel   skin or rind of a fruit such as banana or orange; to strip away or pare: *peel potatoes*

pearl   a gem; yellowish white color
purl   to knit with a purl stitch; to edge with lace or embroidery

pedal   a foot-operated lever: *Put the pedal to the metal.*
peddle   to carry around to sell; to deal out or distribute: *peddle newspapers*

peer   to look intently: *peer in the window*; a person with equal status, class, or age: *a jury of his peers*
pier   a platform on pillars extending from shore over water: *Part of the pier was washed out in the storm.*

penal   pertaining, or subject to punishment, as for crimes or offenses; *a penal offense*
penile   of or concerning the penis: *penile implant*

per   to, for, or by each: *one ticket per person*; according to: *per our agreement*
purr   soft, vibrant sound made by a cat: *She will sit in my lap and purr.*

perceptive   discerning, sensitive, keen, astute; showing insight or intuition: *a perceptive analysis of the challenges*
preceptive   of or expressing a principle or rule regarding conduct; didactic; mandatory; instructive: *a preceptive notice*

peremptory   arbitrary, dogmatic, domineering; imperative: *a peremptory order*; imperious or dictatorial; assertive: *a peremptory manner*
preemptive   an action that is taken before an adversary can act: *a preemptive strike*

preemptory   occupation of land to establish a prior right to buy: *preemptory claim*; an act or statement that is absolute; it cannot be denied: *a preemptory challenge*

perfect   complete; unblemished; faultless: *a perfect performance*
prefect   a person appointed to a position of command or authority; a chief magistrate

perform   discharge, execute, transact; carry out; act, play, or sing: *The rock star performs before an audience of thousands each time he appears.*; fulfill a command: *perform one's duties*
preform   to shape or fashion beforehand; to decide beforehand: *preform an opinion*

perpetrate   to commit: *perpetrate a crime*; to present or execute in a tasteless manner: *perpetrate a poor performance*
perpetuate   save, maintain, sustain; preserve from oblivion: *perpetuate a little-known opera*

perquisite   an extra profit; privilege, or allowance in addition to a main income: *perquisite payment in stock options*; a customary privilege, such as a gratuity or tip
prerequisite   something required as a precondition: *Passing the exam is a prerequisite for college admission.*

persecute   hound; afflict; torture; torment; badger; bother: *persecute the opposition*
prosecute   to institute legal proceedings against: *prosecute the suspect*; carry forward something begun: *prosecute a war*

personal   relating to a particular person; private: *a personal matter*
personnel   body of persons employed in an organization or business: *personnel department*

perspective   a mental view; the state of one's ideas; vista: *It looks good from my perspective.*

prospective   expected; anticipated; future: *prospective earnings*

perspicacious   discerning; perceptive: *a perspicacious observation*; acute; shrewd; penetrating

perspicuous   clearly expressed; lucid, plain, distinct: *perspicuous building*, explicit, intelligible: *an intelligible report*

peruse   read through thoroughly; examine in detail: *peruse a map*

pursue   trail, hunt; follow close upon: *pursue the escapee*; continue to discuss or study: *pursue the options*; go on with: *pursue an education*

pervade   diffuse; fill; spread throughout all parts of: *Suspicion pervades the whole department.*

purvey   furnish; provide; supply: *The caterer will purvey the tables and chairs in addition to the food.*

physic   laxative; cathartic; any medicine; relieve or cure: *The physic made me feel better.*

physique   bodily structure, development, or appearance of an individual: *an athletic physique*

picaresque   a style of fiction dealing with the episodic adventures of rogues; pertaining to or resembling rogues

picturesque   beautiful or striking as in a picture: *a picturesque scene*; strikingly graphic; vivid: *picturesque speech*

picture   a work of art, as a painting, drawing, photograph, etc.; portrait; movie; any visual image; a person or thing resembling another closely: *the very picture of her mother*

pitcher   a container for holding and pouring liquids: *a pitcher of cream*; a person who pitches: *a baseball pitcher*

pinion   the outer part of a bird's wing; a small toothed gear engaging with a larger one
piñon   a pine bearing edible seeds; a type of pine nut

pistil   the female organs of a flower consisting of the stigma, style, and ovary
pistol   a small hand-held firearm

pitiable   lamentable, wretched: *a pitiable hovel*
pitiful   evoking or deserving pity: *a pitiful leper*
piteous   that which exhibits suffering and misery: *piteous poverty*

plain   simple; clearly evident; unpretentious; unadorned: *plain truth*
plane   a carpenter's tool; to smooth: *plane the wood*; to travel by airplane

plaintiff   the party who institutes a suit in court, opposed to defendant
plaintive   expressing sorrow; mournful: *a plaintive melody*; wistful, sad

plait   to braid: *plait the child's hair*
plate   a flat, thin object; a shallow dish; to coat with a layer of metal: *plate with silver*

plantar   of or relating to the sole of the foot: *a plantar wart*
planter   one who cultivates the soil; a large container for plants; the owner or manager of a plantation: *a wealthy Southern planter*

pleas   appeals, entreaties: *pleas for clemency*; excuses; pretexts; a defendant's answers to legal charges
please   be agreeable to; give pleasure: *please the audience*; like or wish: *do what you please*

pleural   pertaining to the pleura, a serous membrane lining the thorax and

enveloping the lungs: *pleural pneumonia*
plural   more than one in number; a plural word or form: *dictionaries is the plural form of dictionary*

plum   an oval, fleshy, edible fruit: *He stuck in his thumb and pulled out a plum.*
plumb   exactly vertical: *plumb in the center*; determine the depth of; experience in extremes: *plumb the depths of fear*; provide with plumbing; work as a plumber
plume   a soft, fluffy feather: *the plume of an egret*; emissions from a stack, flue, or chimney: *a plume of smoke*

polar   pertaining to the North or South Pole: *polar bear*; having magnetic polarity; directly opposite in character or tendency
poller   one who takes samples of opinions on a subject

pole   a long cylindrical piece of wood or metal: *fishing pole*; inside lane of a racetrack: pole position
poll   the casting of votes; a survey of opinions; top or back of the head

poor   needy; penniless; destitute; poverty-stricken
pore   read with attention; a minute orifice as in the skin
pour   rain heavily; send a liquid flowing: *pour coffee*

poplar   a tree
popular   favorably regarded, well-liked; representing the people, common: *popular belief*

populace   the common people; a population
populous   having many people; numerous; crowded

portend   foreshadow as an omen; signify; foretell; forecast; forebode: *The skies portend a possible hurricane.*
pretend   make believe; deceive; feign: *pretend surprise*; simulate, fake, sham, counterfeit; assume: *pretend a title*

portent   augury, warning, sign: *portent of things to come*

potent   strong, mighty, powerful: *potent medicine*; persuasive, influential: *a potent argument*

portion   a part of a whole; section: *A portion of the building was under construction.*; segment; ration; allotment

potion   elixir, brew, concoction; a drink, esp. one having magical powers: *a love potion*

poser   a person who poses, as for a picture

poseur   a person who tries to impress others by behaving affectedly

practicable   workable, achievable, attainable; feasible: *a practicable solution to the problem*

practical   pragmatic; suited to actual conditions; useful; sensible: *a practical person*

praise   glorify, exalt; acclamation, approbation, compliment; laud: *Her performance received praise from all the critics.*

prays   makes a fervent request; beseeches; implores; offers a prayer to a deity: *prays for guidance*

preys   victimizes: *preys upon the poor*

precede   to go before; to preface: *precede a statement with a qualification*

proceed   progress, emanate, ensue; move or go forward; to carry on: *proceed to the exit*

precedence   priority in time, order, or importance; the right to precede others on formal occasions

precedents   previous cases or legal decisions taken as a guide or justification for subsequent cases; example, model, pattern, standard

precession   the act of preceding; precedence; the slow, conical motion of the earth's axis of rotation

procession   a line of people, animals, vehicles, etc., moving along in orderly succession

precipitant   falling headlong; rushing hastily onward; unduly sudden: *precipitant decision*

precipitate   hasten the occurrence of; to cast, plunge, or send violently; accelerate: *precipitate a fight*

precipitous   extremely steep; abrupt, sheer: *a precipitous slope*

precocious   prematurely developed in some faculty or characteristic: *a precocious child*

preconscious   occurring prior to the development of consciousness; the preconscious portion of the mind

prepose   to place (a grammatical form) before a related grammatical form: *The adverb "out" of "put the light out" is preposed in "put out the light."*

propose   to offer a matter for consideration; suggest: *He proposed an item for the agenda.*; to make an offer: *propose marriage*; proffer, tender, present

preposition   a word governing and usually preceding a noun or pronoun and expressing a relation to another word or element; examples of prepositions are *in, on, by, to, from, since, for, of: Where did you come from? What shelf did you put it on? That's what it's for.*

proposition   a proposal; a suggestion of something to be considered, adopted, etc.: *a proposition of marriage or sexual relations*

prescribe   appoint; to order a medicine: *prescribe a painkiller*

proscribe   prohibit, censure, repudiate; to banish: *proscribe drinking in a public park*

presence   the state of being present: *Your presence is requested at the meeting.*; a person's bearing or force of personality: *His presence was commanding.*

presents   gifts: *The child received a lot of presents.*; things presented: *The company presents its new president.*

presentiment   foreboding; a vague expectation: *I had a presentiment that there would be an accident.*

presentment   an act or manner of presenting; the act of presenting information: *The principal made the presentment.*

pretense   pretending or feigning: *a pretense of listening*; a false show of something: *his sympathy was only a pretense*; an allegation or claim: *get a loan under false pretenses*; shamming; semblance; mask, veil

pretext   something put forward to conceal a true purpose; an ostensible reason; excuse: *The leaders used presumed threats as a pretext to declare war.*; subterfuge; evasion

preview   the showing of a movie, play, etc. prior to its public opening; to see or show in advance: *They always show previews before the movie.*

purview   the scope or range of something; responsibility, compass, extent: *The job is within his purview.*

pride   conceit, self-esteem, egotism, vanity; feeling proud; the best of a group: *The pride of the Yankees.*; a group of lions

pried   inquired presumptuously into something: *pried into her personal life*; opened by using leverage: *pried open the cover of the manhole*

prince   a male sovereign or monarch; the chief or greatest: *the prince of journalists*

prints   copies of a photograph or document; fingerprints, paw prints; produces a copy of something on paper or other material

principal   main; foremost; the person in charge: *the school principal*; a capital sum (of money)

principle   essential quality; law; moral rule: *true to her principles*; doctrine: *the principle of the matter*

prodigy   a person with exceptional talent or ability: *a child prodigy*; a
marvelous thing

protégé   a person under the protection, patronage, or tutelage of another: *a
protégé of the concertmaster*

profit   gain; benefit; income from investments or property: *The sale made a
profit.*

prophet   soothsayer; predictor: *prophet of doom*

prophecy   a prediction; the inspired utterance of a prophet: *His prophecy
was that the world would come to an end soon.*

prophesy   to speak as a prophet; to foretell future events: *He will prophesy the
next world war.*

prostate   of or pertaining to the prostate gland

prostrate   prone, supine, incumbent; to lay flat as on the ground; to reduce
to physical weakness

protean   extremely variable; changeable in shape or form, as an amoeba; a
versatile actor

protein   plants or animal compounds rich in amino acids required for
growth and repair of animal tissue

put   to place, set; to assign, attribute

putt   to hit a golf ball with a light stroke

pyretic   of, for, or producing a fever

pyrrhic   (of a victory) won at too great a cost to be of use by the victor; a
metrical foot of two short or unaccented syllables

Q

quail   lose heart or courage; recoil; flinch; cower: *quail in the face of danger*

quake   shake or tremble; shudder: *quake with fear of the monster*

qualm   uneasy feeling; pang of conscience; misgiving: *She has no qualms about lying to her parents.*

queasy   troubled; anxious; worried; nauseated; upset: *After she ate the spoiled food she felt queasy.*

quarts   measures of dry or liquid volume

quartz   a hard, crystalline mineral

quiet   still; soothing; hushed; calm: *quiet the animals*

quit   stop, cease, surrender, release, resign: *quit the job*

quite   very; to a degree; rather: *quite a lovely compliment*

R

rack   framework; spread out; torture: *they put the prisoner on the rack*

wrack   damage or destruction: *wrack and ruin*

rain   water falling to earth in drops: *Soon it's going to rain.*

reign   exercise of sovereign power; widespread influence: *He reigns supreme.*

rein   a leather strap fastened to the bit of a bridle; a means of restraint: *Rein in your anger.*

raise   lift, build, or erect: *The whole community helped them raise the house.*

rays   narrow beams of light; traces of an enlightening influence: *rays of hope*

raze   tear down or demolish: *It took a demolition crew to raze the hotel.*

rap   a knock; a short tapping sound; blame, censure: *take the rap*; conversation; a rhythmical, rhyming monologue recited to music; a small amount, the least bit: *I don't give a rap.*

wrap   enclose something in cloth or paper: *wrap a gift*; the end of filming or taping of a show or scene: *That's a wrap.*

rappel   technique of controlled descent from a height: *rappel down a cliff*
repel   drive back; ward off: *repel the enemy*; be repulsive to

rapt   deeply moved; enraptured; engrossed
wrapped   covered, enveloped, or encased

raptor   one who seizes by force; robber; a raptorial bird
rapture   ecstatic joy; bliss; beatitude

ravage   wreak great destruction or devastation: *ravage the enemy camp*
ravish   abduct, rape, or carry away with emotion: *ravish the young women*

read   reproduce written words mentally or utter them aloud: *read a book*; to apprehend the meaning; assume as intended or deducible: *read too much into a letter*; determine what is being said by the movement of a person's lips: *read lips*

reed   a marsh plant with a firm stem; the vibrating part of the mouthpiece of some wind instruments

real   true; existing; actual: *the real reason*
reel   winding device; a spool; a dance: *danced the Virginia Reel*

reality   what is real or existent; resemblance to what is real: *reality show*; something that constitutes an actual thing: *The reality is that he is your son.*

realty   real property or real estate: *She's a realty salesperson.*

rebuff   blunt or abrupt rejection; snub; spurn: *rebuff a proposal or invitation*

rebuke   a sharp, stern disapproval of; reprove; reprimand; censure; admonish; reproach: *rebuke his bad behavior*

rebut   to argue to the contrary; disprove; confute: *rebut an argument*

receipt   the state of being received into one's possession: *receipt of goods*; a written acknowledgment of payment: *a receipt for the order*

recipe   a set of instructions for making something: *a recipe for muffins*; a device for achieving something: *a recipe for success*

regime   a system of government; a mode of rule: *a dictatorial regime*

regimen   regulated course, as of diet or exercise: *a health regimen*

regiment   a military unit of ground forces: *He sent three regiments into battle.*

reluctant   disinclined; unwilling to act: *She's reluctant to report him to the police.*

reticent   unwilling to speak; reserved; taciturn, uncommunicative: *She was reticent to answer our questions.*

reprisal   retaliation against an enemy; redress; revenge

reprise   to repeat; in music: a return to the first theme

reprobate   scoundrel; wastrel; rogue; outcast: *The ex-con is a worthless reprobate.*

reprobation   disapproval, condemnation or censure; rejection: *She expressed her reprobation of the proposal.*

repudiate   to reject as having no authority; disown; reject with disapproval; renounce: *repudiate a leader*

repugn   to oppose or refute: *repugn the candidate*

repulse   to drive back; repel; rebuff, snub, shun: *repulse a man's advances*

requirement   demanded in accordance with set regulations: *A degree is a requirement for the job.*

requisite   something that circumstances make necessary: *A cool head is a requisite for a police officer.*

rescind   countermand, repeal, veto; nullify, retract: *rescind an agreement*
resend   send again; send back: *resend a letter*

residence   habitation, domicile; stay, sojourn; the place in which a person resides: *My residence is within the city limits.*
residents   physicians who are   in full-time attendance in a hospital and who often live on the premises; those who reside in a place: *residents of a condominium complex*

respectably   honorably; suitably: *He performed his job respectably.*
respectfully   full of respect; with regard: *She listened respectfully to his advice.*
respectively   sequentially; in precisely the order given: *John and Hal finished first and second, respectively.*

rest   abstain or be relieved from exertion: *Rest here awhile before traveling on.*; left without further investigation: *Let the matter rest.*
wrest   to usurp forcefully; to extract by guile or persistence: *wrest a confession from the suspect*

restive   nervous, unquiet; recalcitrant, disobedient, obstinate, balky: *a restive horse*
restless   agitated, fretful, without rest: *restless night*

retch   to make efforts to vomit
wretch   an unfortunate or unhappy person

right   correct; proper; just; appropriate: *the right way*
rite   religious ceremony; ceremonial act: *marriage rite*

role   a part played by an actor; a function: *the role of a wife*
roll   to turn; to throw as in dice; a small bread

root   part of a plant normally below the ground; basic cause, source, or origin: *the root of the problem*
route   a way or course taken: *the shortest route to your destination*; a round traveled in delivering, selling, or collecting goods: *a newspaper route*

rote   mechanical or habitual repetition: *Try to learn your multiplication table by rote.*
wrote   past tense of write: *I wrote a letter to you.*

S

---

sail   a piece of canvas or other fabric extended on rigging to catch the wind and propel a sailing vessel; an apparatus that catches the wind on a windmill; to move along or travel over water
sale   the act of selling; the amount sold; disposal of goods at reduced prices; an event where goods are sold; a public auction

salvage   the rescue of a ship and its cargo from loss at sea; the property saved in such a way; the act of saving anything from a wreck, fire, etc.
selvage   an edging that prevents cloth from unraveling

sanatorium   a hospital for the treatment of chronic diseases, such as tuberculosis or mental disorders
sanitarium   an institution for the preservation or recovery of health; a convalescent hospital; a health resort
sanitarian   clean and wholesome; a specialist in public sanitation and health

satire   the use of ridicule, irony, sarcasm, etc., to expose folly or vice or to lampoon someone; burlesque, caricature, parody

satyr one of a class of Greek woodland gods with a goat's or horse's ears and tail and budding horns; a lustful or sensual man; lecher

saver a person who saves, especially money

savior a person who saves from danger or destruction, one who rescues or delivers

savor a characteristic taste, flavor, etc.; to appreciate or enjoy the taste of; to enjoy an experience

scene the place where events in real life, drama, or fiction occur: *scene of the crime*; any view or picture; an embarrassing public display of emotion: *Please don't make a scene!*

seen past participle of *see*: *I have seen the light.*

scrip a certificate to be exchanged for goods or cash

script handwriting; the text of a play, TV program, or motion picture

scull either of a pair of small oars used by a single rower; a small boat propelled by a scull or a pair of sculls

skull the skeleton of the head

sculptor an artist who makes sculptures

sculpture the art of making forms by chiseling, carving, modeling, casting, etc.

sea ocean; overwhelming quantity: *a sea of troubles*

see to perceive with the eyes; to perceive mentally: *I see your point.*

seasonable timely; fit; appropriate; characteristic of the season: *seasonable weather*

seasonal pertaining to the seasons of the year; periodical: *seasonal work*; depending or occurring on the season: *seasonal fluctuations in rainfall*

sees   perceives with the eyes, views; recognizes, visits

seise   *chiefly law:* to take into legal custody; confiscate

seize   take hold of suddenly and forcibly; grab; overwhelm; to take possession by force

sensibility   capacity for feeling; responsiveness: *She has a great sensibility for her patients.*

sensitivity   ability to react to stimuli: *sensitivity to light*

sensual   carnal; lascivious; lacking moral restraints: *a sensual dance*

sensuous   affecting the senses: *sensuous poetry;* sensible; sentient

serf   a person in a condition of servitude; vassal, peasant

surf   the swell of the sea breaking on shore or reefs; the foam produced by this; to ride the surf as with a surfboard; to search through a computer network for information: *surf the Web*

serge   a twilled woolen fabric: *His serge suit was shiny from many years of wear.*

surge   a rolling swell of water: *The huge surge of the sea frightened us.;* a rush of current in a circuit: *I need a surge protector for my computer.;* any sudden or abrupt strong increase

sew   fasten by stitches made with needle and thread; make clothes with cloth: *She will sew a party dress for me.*

so   in the way or manner indicated; in order that: *Please RSVP so that we'll know how many reservations to make.;* to the extent or degree indicated: *I feel so good.*

sow   scatter seed on the earth; to plant: *sow a crop;* circulate

sewn   made, repaired: *I have sewn the pieces together.*

sown   impregnated with seed; propagated; spread: *You have sown the seeds of suspicion.*

shear to clip or cut; remove hair or fleece from: *shear the sheep*
sheer thin; fine; transparent; steep: *a sheer nightgown*

shone past tense of shine: *Today is cloudy, but yesterday the sun shone.*
shown past participle of show: *A link has been shown between obesity and diabetes.*

shudder to tremble from horror, fear, or cold; quiver; shiver: *I shudder to think how close I came to having a terrible accident.*
shutter a movable cover for an opening; a device for opening or closing the aperture of a camera lens; to close down: *Shutter the cottage for the winter.*

sight vision: *My sight has been getting dimmer.*; something worth seeing: *a sight for sore eyes*
site location; setting of an event: *This is the site where we will build our dream home.*

slay murder; slaughter; assassinate: *They planned to slay the King.*
sleigh a light vehicle on runners; a sled: *a one-horse open sleigh*
sley the reed of a loom; the warp count in woven fabrics

sleight skill; dexterity; stratagem; legerdemain: *sleight of hand*
slight small in size, degree, or amount; delicate; act of disrespect: *He reacted with anger to the slight.*

sloe fruit of the blackthorn; the shrub itself
slow unhurried; gradual; leisurely

soar rise, fly, or glide without effort: *The eagles soar high into the sky.*
sore painful to the touch; tender: *a sore arm*; open wound

soared rose into the air; rose rapidly; flew a plane that has no engine

sword   a thrusting weapon with a long, sharp-pointed blade: *They fought with swords.*

sol   *music:* the fifth tone of a diatonic scale; a Peruvian coin
Sol   ancient Roman god personifying the sun

sole   only, unique; the undersurface of a foot or shoe; a flatfish
soul   spirit, heart, essence, core

some time   a little time; a short while: *I need some time away from my business.*
sometime   at an unstated or indefinite time: *Come up and see me sometime.*
sometimes   now and then, at times: *Sometimes I prefer the beach in the winter.*

some   remarkable: *That was some thunder storm.*; unspecified quantity: *I'd like some candy.*
sum   a quantity obtained by addition: *The sum of 13 and 20 is 33.*; the final aggregate

son   a male human offspring: *My dad always wanted a son.*
sun   a star that is the source of light and heat for planets in the solar system; the luminous celestial body the earth and other planets revolve around: *We warmed ourselves in the sun.*

soot   a black substance rising in fine flakes in smoke
suit   a legal action; a matched set of clothes; meet the requirements of: *This room will suit me just fine.*

spacious   large in expanse or scope; roomy: *a spacious auditorium*
specious   plausible but false; based on pretense; deceptively pleasing: *His incorrect conclusion arose from specious reasoning.*

spiritual   concerned with sacred or religious things; refined; sensitive: *She is a spiritual woman.*

spirituous   distilled, as whiskey; containing much alcohol: *a spirituous concoction*

splutter   speak in a vehement or choking manner; utter rapidly or incoherently, spatter, as a liquid; noise or fuss; a blend of the words *splash* and *sputter*

sputter   make popping or sizzling sounds; to eject particles of saliva or food from the mouth explosively and involuntarily; some of the same definitions as for splutter, such as to utter incoherently

staff   a pole or stick; personnel: *The entire staff will attend the conference.*

staph   staphylococcus, a parasitic bacteria: *a staph infection*

staid   sober and sedate; characterized by dignity and propriety: *a staid professor*

stayed   continuing or remaining in a place; a judicial order forbidding an action until the order is lifted: *stayed the execution*

stair   step or flight of steps: *walk up the stairs*

stare   steady gaze; to look at intently: *It's not polite to stare.*

stake   a stick or post; wager; bet: *I have a stake in that race.*

steak   a slice of meat or fish: *I'll have my steak rare.*

stammer   speak with involuntary breaks and pauses or with spasmodic repetitions of syllables or sounds; pause, hesitate, falter

stutter   speak in such a way that the rhythm is interrupted by repetition, blocks, or spasms, or prolongations of sounds and syllables along with contortions of the face and body; distorted speech

[Both *stammer* and *stutter* mean to speak with difficulty. *Stammer* suggests inarticulate sounds or interrupted speech caused by excitement, embarrassment, confusion, or other emotion that may require special treatment to correct. *Stutter* designates a broad range of speech defects. It is the term that is preferred in technical usage: *His stutter was more than merely a stammer of embarrassment.*]

stance   position of the body while standing; a mental or emotional position: *take a firm stance*

stanch   to stop the flow of blood or other liquid: *Use direct pressure to stanch the bleeding.*

staunch   constant; true; faithful; steadfast: *a staunch friend*; strong; substantial

stationary   fixed; standing still; not movable; not changing: *Inflation has remained stationary.*

stationery   writing paper; writing materials: *I ordered personalized stationery.*

statue   image of human or animal carved in marble or bronze: *There is a statue of the local hero in the center of town.*

stature   height or uprightness: *He was of unusual stature.*

statute   a law enacted by the legislative branch of a government: *The maximum allowable speed was established by statute.*

steal   to take the property of another without permission: *Did he steal your purse?*

steel   modified form of iron: *The building is reinforced with steel beams.*

stele   stone marker or monument: *An ancient stele marked the grave.*

steer   to guide or direct the course of; a young ox castrated and raised for beef

stere   a unit of volume equal to one cubic meter

straight   having no waves or bends: *a straight path to the beach*; candid and direct: *straight talk*; unmixed: *I drink my whiskey straight.*

strait   (often straits) a narrow passage of water connecting two large bodies of water; difficulty; distress: *dire straits*

stricter   more rigid or exacting in enforcing rules: *stricter parents*
stricture   a restriction; an adverse criticism: *The critic made a stricture regarding the script.*

subset   a set that is part of a larger set
subtext   underlying or implicit meaning, as of a literary work: *What is the subtext of the story?*
subtype   a subordinate type; a special type included in a more general type

subtitle   a secondary and usually explanatory title, as in a literary work
subtopic   one of the divisions into which a main topic may be divided

success   favorable or prosperous outcome; attainment of wealth, position, fame, etc.
succuss   to shake up; shake

suite   matched furniture: *a bedroom suite*; connected rooms: *The suite contains a sitting room, two bedrooms, and two baths.*
sweet   the taste experience of sugar; a food rich in sugar; pleasing to the mind or feelings: *a sweet deal*; in an affectionate manner: *You are very sweet to me.*

summary   a brief account of the main points of something; outline, précis, synopsis: *Please provide a summary of the book.*
summery   like summer: *a bright summery day*

suspension   something that is suspended or hung; temporary withholding of a privilege: *I got a suspension for yelling at the teacher.*; decision, etc.; interruption, discontinuance, abeyance
suspicion   the act of suspecting; doubt, mistrust, misgiving: *I have a suspicion that she isn't being truthful.*

T

tacked   changed a boat's heading relative to the wind; fastened with a short nail with a sharp point and large head; sewed together loosely with large stitches: *tacked the hem of the dress*

tact   sensitive perception of what is appropriate in dealing with others: *The director has a lot of tact.*

tacks   short, sharp nails with broad, flat heads; fastens; zigzags

tax   a sum of money demanded by a government; levy; lay a burden on; strain, stretch

tail   the prolongation of an animal's rear end: *The dog wagged his tail.*; the rear part of an aircraft; the side of a coin that does not bear a head or date; someone employed to follow and report the movements of another: *put a tail on the suspect*

tale   story; an actual or fictitious narrative of an event: *He told an exciting tale.*

tankard   large drinking cup, often with a handle and hinged cover: *a tankard of ale*

tanker   a ship, airplane, or truck used for bulk shipment of liquids or gasses; a tank trailer or tank truck

taper   a slender candle; a gradual decrease: *The storm will taper off soon.*

tapir   animal resembling swine

taught   past tense of teach: *He taught me to sing.*

taut   trim; tidy; tense: *She speaks in short, taut sentences.*

team   two or more who work together or play on the same side as in a game: *She's on my team.*

teem   to be full of; swarm; abound: *The area teems with bees.*

tear   (tear as in teardrop) a drop of the saline solution that is secreted by the lacrimal glands: *I won't shed a tear if you go.*
tier   row, rank, or layer, one atop the other: *Their seats are on the third tier.*

tremblor   a tremor; earthquake
trembler   a person or thing that trembles

tenant   occupant; one who holds the right to occupy a place: *The tenant of that apartment is a woman.*
tenet   principle, belief, doctrine; part of a body of doctrine: *tenet of a church*

tense   stretched tight; high-strung: *She is overly tense.*; a category of verbal inflection
tents   portable canvas shelters: *The homeless are living in tents by the river.*
tints   a color or variety of color; hue: *Use pastel tints for the walls.*

than   used after comparative words such as other: *She is prettier than her sister.*
then   at that time: *He'll be home then.*; soon afterward: *Then we'll have dinner.*; next in order

their   possessive case of *they: It is their book.*
there   in or at that place: *The book is over there.*
they're   they are: *They're working on a second edition.*

threw   past tense of throw; hurl; cast; emit; project: *She threw the ball a long way.*
through   by way of: *We'll be driving through Seattle.*; finished: *We'll be through with the project by tonight.*

throe, throes   a violent spasm or pain: *the throes of childbirth*; a sharp attack
   of emotion; tumult; chaos; turmoil

throw   fling, launch, send: *throw the ball*

throne   the chair occupied by a sovereign or other exalted person on
   ceremonial occasions

thrown   projected; propelled; hurled: *He has been thrown into prison.*

tide   periodic rise and fall of the ocean: *High tide is at 6:03 p.m.*; a current,
   tendency, or drift, as of events: *A tide of fear could lead to war.*

tied   bound, fastened, or attached with a rope or string drawn together and
   knotted: *He tied the package securely.*

tiered   arranged in tiers: *a five-tiered wedding cake*

tired   weary, fatigued: *I'm tired from a long day at work.*

timber   wood, especially when suitable for building purposes: *Stack the
   timber next to the house.*

timbre   the characteristic quality of a sound: *The timbre of his voice was
   unique.*

to   toward, on, against, upon

too   also: *me too*; excessive: *too much*

two   a number: *Take two; they're small.*

toe   a digit on the foot of certain mammals: *He stubbed his toe.*

tow   pull or haul by a rope, chain, or other device: *They had to tow my car.*

tortuous   circuitous; devious; full of twists, turns, or bends: *a tortuous road
   up the mountain*

torturous   pertains to suffering: *We toil in the torturous heat.*

tracked   followed the traces of; made tracks upon: *The children tracked mud
   into the house.*

tract   pamphlet or leaflet; an extended area of land: *a housing tract*

transcendent   surpassing all others; pre-eminent: *Her beauty was transcendent.*
transcendental   mystical; knowledge derived from intuitive sources: *It was a transcendental experience.*

translucent   permitting light to pass through but diffusing it so that objects are not clearly visible: *a translucent lampshade*; lucid: *a translucent description*
transparent   allows objects to be seen clearly through it: *clear water is transparent*; crystalline

treaties   formal agreements; formal documents embodying an agreement; compacts
treatise   formal exposition in writing of the principles of a subject, more detailed than an essay

triad   a group of three, as notes in a chord
triage   sorting according to quality; the assignment of degrees of urgency to decide the order of treatment of injuries, illnesses, etc.

trooper   soldier or police officer: *He was a state trooper.*
trouper   actor; dependable person: *He's always on time—a real trouper.*

trustee   a person who is given control of another's property: *He is the trustee of his mother's estate.*
trusty   a prisoner given special privileges: *The trusty works on the landscape outside the prison walls.*

turbid   cloudy, muddy, murky: *The turbid water overflowed the banks of the river.*

turgid   swollen, distended, overblown, pompous: *The politician was known for his turgid prose.*

U

---

udder   a mammary gland, especially when baggy and with more than one teat, as in cows

utter   speak or pronounce: *Don't utter a word.*; complete; total; absolute: *the utter truth*; unconditional; unqualified: *He's an utter liar.*

unaware   not aware or cognizant: *He was unaware of the danger lurking.*

unawares   unexpectedly, without forethought, by surprise: *Her anger caught him unawares.*

underserved   those whose needs are not sufficiently served: *underserved children of the ghetto*

undeserved   not justly or rightly earned or merited: *an undeserved reward*

undo   reverse or erase; annul; untie; unwrap: *undo a knot*

undue   exceeding the appropriate or normal; excessive: *the use of undue force*

unreal   not actual; imaginary, fanciful, delusory; lacking in truth; not genuine; false; sham

unreel   to unwind from a reel

urban   relating to a city; characteristic of city life: *There are many benefits to urban living.*

urbane   polished and elegant in manner or style; suave; cosmopolitan: *He has a sophisticated, urbane way about him.*

[*Urban* and *urbane* once meant the same thing: *belonging to a city.* Both words are derived from the Latin *urbanis*. Later, *urbane* developed the more specialized sense of *refined, polite,* and *elegant,* which were considered to be characteristics of those who lived in cities rather than those living in the country.]

V

vain excessively proud of one's appearance, qualities, etc.; conceited: *She is very vain about her long black hair.*; arrogant; egotistical; without effect or avail: *Her efforts were in vain.*; worthless; unimportant

vane blade in a wheel moved by air, steam, or water: *A weather vane shows the direction of the wind.*; someone who is changeable or fickle

vein blood vessel; a natural channel; a body or stratum of ore: *a rich vein of coal*; a condition, mood, or temper: *a vein of sadness*; tone; touch; thread; streak

vale a valley; the world, or mortal or earthly life: *this vale of tears*

veil a piece of netting worn by women for concealment; something that covers or screens: *a veil of smoke*

vary to be different; modify; deviate: *Her actions seem to vary from the norm.*

very to a high degree; extremely: *a very important matter*

vassal dependent; bondman; servant; slave: *The vassal cared for the entire cornfield.*

vessel container; water craft; airship: *The new boat was a seaworthy vessel.*

venal open to bribery; mercenary; corruptible: *a venal administration prone to greed and deception*

venial pardonable; trifling; not seriously wrong: *His outburst in class was only a venial offense.*

veracity truthfulness: *He has a reputation for veracity and we can trust what he says.*

voracity excessive eagerness, greediness, great hunger: *He gobbled down his food with voracity.*

verses   stanzas; poems or pieces of poetry: *She recited verses from her latest poem.*

versus   against; as compared to; in contrast with: *a partial compromise versus total defeat*

vial   a small container used for liquids: *The biology student held up a vial of swamp water.*

vile   disgusting; loathsome; depraved: *He's a vile man with a cruel streak.*

viol   a stringed musical instrument: *He was the finest viol player in the orchestra.*

violation   a breach, infringement, or transgression as of a law or rule: *She was stopped for a traffic violation.*

volition   a choice or decision made by the will; discretion: *She left on her own volition.*

vice   a bad habit; serious moral failing: *Drinking too much is a vice.*

vise   a clamp for holding metal or wood in place: *I used a vise to hold the wood as I sawed it in half.*

W

wail   moan or lament; to cry loudly: *The toddler is sure to wail when his mother leaves.*

whale   hit, beat, strike hard: *whale away at the bully*; a very large cetacean

waist   the narrow middle part of an object: *She wore a sash at her waist.*

waste   to use carelessly; lose; squander: *It's not good to waste food.*

wait   postpone; linger; remain; stay: *Wait with me for the bus.*

weight   measurement of heaviness or mass: *I was dismayed by how much weight I had gained.*

waive   relinquish a right voluntarily: *waive his right to a jury trial*; dispense with; forgo: *waive a fee*

wave   surf; whitecap; undulate: *wave a flag*; to signal with the hand: *wave good-bye*

waiver   intentional relinquishment of a right; the document that evidences a waiver: *She signed a waiver.*

waver   vacillate; fluctuate; hesitate; falter; sway: *She wanted to go, but her doubts made her waver.*

wander   rove, ramble, move about without a fixed course: *He tends to wander aimlessly throughout the city.*

wonder   something that causes feelings of wonder; feelings aroused by a marvel; to query in the mind: *Sometimes we wonder what we're here for.*

wangle   maneuver, finagle, wheedle: *wangle an invitation*

wrangle   to argue or dispute; an altercation; to round up cattle, horses, or other livestock

want   to desire greatly; need; lack: *I really want a new car.*

wont   accustomed to; apt or likely: *He is wont to make mistakes when he hurries.*

won't   will not: *I won't be able to go with you.*

ware   pottery or ceramics: *She sells her wares at street festivals*; a specified kind of merchandise: *silverware, glassware*

wear   to have on: *he will wear a uniform*; carry; display; waste; depreciate: *wear and tear*

warrantee   a person to whom a warranty is made: *The customer is the warrantee.*

warranty   authorization; assurance of quality: *I got a one-year warranty on the machine.*

way   the condition of things; how something is done or how it happens; a pathway: *This is the way you get to the pool.*

weigh   determine the weight of something; to ponder and consider: *Weigh your decision before going forward.*; to consider one's words carefully: *Weigh your words before you speak.*

weather   meteorological conditions: temperature and wind and clouds and precipitation; face or endure: *I can weather the storm.*

whether   used to introduce the first of two or more alternative conditions: *I haven't decided whether to go or stay.*

weak   not strong; feeble; lacking firmness or force of will: *The illness had made her weak.*

week   a period of seven days: *It has been a week since I saw him.*

weird   involving or suggesting the supernatural: *a weird glowing object in the sky*; fantastic; bizarre: *That's a weird costume you are wearing.*

wired   equipped with wires; made of wire; consisting of or made of wires: *a wired barrier*; connected electronically to computer networks; a feeling of excitement or anticipation; edgy: *You're certainly wired today.*

wench   peasant girl; female servant; wanton woman: *a saucy little wench*

winch   a hoisting machine: *They used a winch to hoist the wrecked cars onto the crusher.*

wrench   a tool with jaws for gripping, turning, or twisting an object: *Sometimes I have to use a wrench to open jars.*

wend   to proceed or go: *She had to wend her way through the crowd.*

wind   (pronounced wīnd) to change direction; meander: *The creek winds through the woods.*

which   an interrogative pronoun, used in questions about alternatives: *Which dessert would you like?*

witch   a female thought to have special powers derived from the devil; a female sorcerer; an ugly evil-looking old woman: *Many fairytales feature a scary witch.*

whirl   rotate or spin rapidly: *The blades of the windmill whirl in the breeze.*
whorl   one of the ridges of a fingerprint; a coil or curl: *whorls of frost on a window*

who   what person or persons: *Who was that woman?*
whom   objective case of *who: To whom are you speaking?*

who's   who is: *Who's going with you?*
whose   possessive case of *which* or *who: Whose comb is this?*

wiggle   move quickly and irregularly from side to side: *The puppy wiggled its tail.*; undulating
wriggle   writhe; squirm; to move by twisting and turning the body, as a worm or snake: *He tried to wriggle out of the narrow opening.*

wood   the hard, fibrous substance of a tree or shrub; the trunks or main stems of trees; timber or lumber: *Most furniture is made out of wood.*
would   past tense and past participle of *will: Would you have gone to the game with me if I had asked you to?*

wreak   to inflict or execute punishment: *wreak revenge*; visit; vent; unleash: *He wreaked his anger on the office staff.*
wreck   destroy; devastate; shatter; tear down: *The mob will wreck the goal posts.*; the remains of something ruined: *The tornado turned the house into a wreck.*

wreath   a circular band of flowers, foliage, or other material, used as an adornment; a garland: *We always put an evergreen wreath on the door for the holidays.*

wreathe   to encircle or adorn, as with a wreath; to envelop: *Her head was wreathed in spring flowers.*

wright   one who constructs something: *a wheelwright; a playwright*
write   pen, author, draft, create, compose: *I write at least three pages every day.*

Y

yoke   a working frame for oxen
yolk   the yellow of an egg

your   belonging to you: *Is this your child?*
you're   you are: *You're going to the party with me.*

Chapter Five

Frequently Misspelled Words

"Do you spell it with a 'V' or a 'W'?" inquired the judge.
"That depends on the taste and fancy of the speller, my Lord," replied Sam.

—CHARLES DICKENS, *PICKWICK PAPERS*

IT IS UNDERSTANDABLE that most of us have trouble spelling correctly. The English language is made up of so many other languages that spelling rules rarely apply. Some new words go through several variations of spelling before they settle into one widely accepted standard, such as *Web site*, which is sometimes spelled *web site* or *website*.

Many British words are spelled differently from American words. Again, this book follows *The Chicago Manual*, which uses American spelling. Some examples are *color* (American) and *colour* (British), *demoralize* and *demoralise*.

Consonant and vowel sounds are not the same as consonant and vowel letters. The *y* at the beginning of a word is a consonant, as in *yes* and *yellow*. But it becomes a vowel when it is at the end of a word: *pretty, fairly*.

Often the *e* at the end of a word does not represent a sound itself but indicates the pronunciation of the preceding vowel, as in *bite*. With the *e* it is a long *i*; without the *e* it is a short *i*. This bit of information won't always help you in your pronunciation because, for example, *hypocrite* and *rite,* should rhyme but don't.

The same combination of letters isn't always pronounced the same, caus-ing us to mispronounce words fairly frequently, which makes it easier to misspell them as well. Historical changes through the years have driven spelling and pronunciation far apart.

An example of this is the letter combination *-ough. Rough* and *tough* are pronounced *ruff* and *tuff. Slough,* when it means a swamp or quagmire, is pro-nounced *slow.* However, when *slough* refers to the skin that an animal casts off or molts, it is pronounced *sluff.*

Ought, thought, and *bought* are pronounced *awt, thawt,* and *bawt. Cough* and *trough* are pronounced *cawf* and *trawf.* Thus, it would make sense that *bough* would be pronounced *bawf.* But no. *Bough* rhymes with *wow.*

It would seem that *through* and *thorough* logically would rhyme with one of the above words but they don't. They don't even rhyme with each other. *Through* rhymes with *true* while *thorough* rhymes with *burrow.*

Words with the letters *eight* in them don't always sound alike either. *Eight, weight,* and *freight* all rhyme with *ate* but *height* and *sleight* rhyme with *ite.* There have been attempts through the years to simplify the spelling of our English words. And it makes sense to have some kind of uniform rule of spelling matching pronunciation in most words. For example, *weight* and *freight* would be spelled *wate* and *frate. Height* and *sleight* would be *hite* and *slite.* But no matter how many times these changes were suggested, they were roundly rejected.

The *i* before *e* rule. There are a few spelling guidelines, as in *ei* and *ie* words. In school, many of us learned the spelling rule of "*i* before *e* except after *c.*" Here is a poem that children used to be taught (and maybe still are) in ele-mentary school:

> I before E
> Except after C,
> Or when sounded as A,
> As in *neighbor* or *weigh.*

Simple enough, except that there are more exceptions than those in the poem. The actual rule is this: *i* always goes before *e* except

(1) after the letter *c,* as in *deceive, receipt,* and *conceit;*
(2) when the sound of the double vowel is an *a,* as in *beige, deign, eight,*

feign, feint, freight, geisha, heinous, heir, reign, reindeer, reins, sleigh, weigh, and *weight;*

(3) in these specific words (not a complete list): *either, neither, feisty, forfeit, Geiger, heifer, height, leisure, seize, seizure, sleight, seismology, seize,* and *weird.*

This rule is probably best forgotten because it will mess you up as often as it will help you.

Words ending in *-ance, -ence, -ant,* **and** *-ent.* Among these words are: *apparent, coherent, appearance, abstinence, superintendent,* and *tenant.* There is no simple, comprehensive spelling rule that applies to words with these endings. You'll have to memorize the spelling of them or look them up every time you write them. Some of these words appear in the list of misspelled words but not all of them because there are far too many.

Words ending in *cede, ceed,* **and** *sede.* When in doubt, spell words ending in these letters with *cede,* as in *concede, intercede, recede,* and *precede,* and you'll be right most of the time. In this rule, all you have to do is memorize the words that *don't* end in *cede* because there are only four. Three of them end in *ceed: exceed, proceed,* and *succeed.* And only one ends in *sede,* and that one is *supersede.*

Words ending in *c.* Here's a fairly reliable rule: with words ending in *c* you add a *k* if you join them with "soft" vowels that would otherwise soften the *c* to an *s* sound. When you add the *k* it keeps the *c* hard. Some examples are *panic, panicking, panicked; picnic, picnicking, picnicked; traffic, trafficking, trafficked.* The plurals are without the *k: panics.*

Other erratic word endings. Frequently misspelled words for which there are no clear-cut rules are words ending in *able* and *ible, er* and *or, eous* and *ious, ise* and *ize,* and *sion* and *tion.*

Plurals. The general rules of plurals are that when a noun ends in a soft *ch* or in *s, sh, j, x,* or *z,* the plural is *es: churches, flashes, fixes.* When it ends in *y* and is preceded by a consonant the plural is formed by replacing the *y* with *ies: babies, thirties, navies.*

Possessives. According to *The Chicago Manual of Style*, "The possessive of singular nouns is formed by the addition of an apostrophe and an *s*, and the possessive of plural nouns (except for a few irregular plurals) by the addition of an apostrophe only." Examples given are *the horse's mouth, the puppies' tails*, and *the children's desk.*

The Manual states, "The general rule for the possessive of nouns covers most proper nouns, including most names ending in sibilants . . .," with some exceptions. Among the examples it gives are *Kansas's, Texas's, Burns's poems, Marx's theories, Berlioz's opera, Ross's land, the Rosses' land, Jones's reputation,* and *the Joneses' reputation.*

Traditional exceptions to the rule are Jesus and Moses: *in Jesus' name* and *Moses' leadership.* Other exceptions are names of more than one syllable with an unaccented ending pronounced *eez*. The possessive *s* is seldom added to these names. Examples include *Euripides' plays, Ramses' tomb,* and *Xerxes' army.*

Often people misspell words because they are confusing them with a word that sounds just like the word they want to use but means something different. (See chapter 4, "Frequently Misused Words.")

A

abacus, not *abbacus*
abandon, not *abanden*
abatement, not *abbatement*
abbreviate, not *abreviate*
abdicate, not *abdacate*
abduction, not *abducksion*
aberration, not *abberation*
abeyance, not *abayence*
abhorrent, not *abhorent*
abject, not *abjeck*
able, not *abel*
abnormality, not *abnormallity*
aboard, not *abored*
abolish, not *abalish*
abominable, not *abaminable*
aborigine, not *abariginie*
abrasion, not *abrazion*
abrasive, not *abrazive*
abrupt, not *abrup*
abscess, not *absess*
abscond, not *abscand*
absence, not *absense*
absolute, not *absalute*
absorbent, not *absorbant*
absorption, not *absorbtion*
abstain, not *abstane*
abstinence, not *abstinance*
abstinent, not *abstinant* or *abstenent*
abstract, not *abstrack*
absurd, not *abserd* or *abzurd*
abundant, not *abundent*
abusive, not *abusave* or *abuseve*
abyss, not *abiss*
academically, not *academicly*

a cappella, not *a capella*
academy, not *accademy*
Acapulco, not *Accapulco*
accelerator, not *accillarator*
accent, not *acsent*
acceptable, not *acceptible*
access, not *acsess*
accessible, not *accessable*
accessory, not *accessary*
accidentally, not *accidently*
acclimate, not *acclamate*
accolade, not *accollade*
accommodate, not *accomodate*
accompany, not *accompeny*
accompaniment, not
    accompanyment
accomplish, not *accomplesh*
accord, not *acord* or *achord*
accordion, not *accordian*
accost, not *acost*
accrue, not *accrew*
accumulate, not *accummulate*
accuracy, not *accuresy* or *acuracy*
accurate, not *acurate*
accursed, not *acursed*
accusation, not *accuzation*
accustom, not *acustom*
acerbic, not *aserbic*
achievement, not *acheivement*
acknowledgment, not
    acknoledgement
achievement, not *acheivement*
acoustic, not *accuestic* or *acustic*
acquaintance, not *acquaintence*
acquiescence, not *acquiesance*
acquire, not *aquire*
acquitted, not *aquitted*
acrimonious, not *acramonious*

acrobat, not *acrabat* or *accrobat*

across, not *accross*

acupressure, not *accupressure*

acupuncture, not *accupuncture*

acrylic, not *accrylic* or *acrilic*

adage, not *addage*

adamant, not *adament*

adaptable, not *adaptible*

addendum, not *adendum*

addict, not *addic* or *adict*

additive, not *addative*

additionally, not *additionaly*

address, not *adress*

adenoids, not *adanoids*

adept, not *addep*

adequate, not *adaquate*

adhere, not *adhear*

adhesive, not *adhezive*

adieu, not *adeiu*

adjacent, not *ajacent*

adjective, not *ajective* or *adjetive*

adjourn, not *ajourn*

adjunct, not *adjunck*

adjutant, not *adjutent*

administer, not *admenister* or
     adminester

admiral, not *admirel*

admirable, not *admerable* or
     admirible

admiration, not *admeration*

admissible, not *admissable*

admission, not *admision*

admittance, not *admitance* or
     admittence

admonish, not *admonesh*

adolescent, not *adolesent*

adorable, not *adorible*

adrenalin, not *addrenalin*

adulterate, not *adultarate*

adultery, not *adultry*

advancement, not *advansement*

advantageous, not *advantagious*

adventurous, not *adventureous*

adversary, not *adversery*

advertisement, not *advertisment*

advisory, not *advisery*

advocate, not *advacate*

aerie, not *airie*

aeronautical, not *aironautical*

affable, not *afable*

affair, not *afair*

affidavit, not *affadavit*

affiliate, not *afiliate*

affirmative, not *affirmitive*

Afghanistan, not *Afganistan*

aficionado, not *aficianado* or
     afficionado

aforementioned, not *aformentioned*

aggravate, not *agravate*

aghast, not *agast*

agnostic, not *agnostick*

agreeable, not *agreable* or
     agreeible

ailment, not *ailmint*

aisle, not *aile*

albatross, not *albotross* or
     albetross

album, not *albem*

albumin, not *albuman*

alcoholic, not *alchololic*

alien, not *alian*

allege, not *alledge*

allegory, not *allagory*

allegro, not *alegro*

alleviate, not *aleviate*

alligator, not *aligator*

allocation, not *alocation*

allotting, not *alloting*

allowance, not *allowence*

alibi, not *allibi*

alimony, not *alamony*

alignment, not *alinement*

already, not *allready*

almanac, not *alminac*

almighty, not *allmighty*

almond, not *almend*

alphabet, not *alphibet*

although, not *allthough*

altitude, not *altatude*

altogether, not *alltogether*

Alzheimer's, not *Altzeimer's*

amateur, not *amatuer*

ambient, not *ambiant*

ambivalence, not *ambivalance*

ambulance, not *ambulence*

ameliorate, not *amelliorate*

amenable, not *amenible*

amendment, not *ammendment*

ammunition, not *amunition*

amorphous, not *ammorphous*

amphitheater, not *ampitheater*

amplify, not *amplefy*

amplitude, not *ampletide*

amulet, not *ammulet*

anachronism, not *anacronism*

analgesic, not *annalgesic*

analogous, not *analogeous*

analogy, not *annalogy*

analyze, not *analize*

ancestor, not *ancester*

ancient, not *anceint*

animosity, not *annimosity*

anesthetic, not *anasthetic*

animation, not *anamation*

annihilate, not *anniolate*

annuity, not *anuity*

anonymous, not *anonimous*

antarctic, not *antartic*

antecedent, not *antecedant*

antelope, not *antalope*

antiperspirant, not *antiperspirent*

aperture, not *apperture*

aphorism, not *aforism*

aphrodisiac, not *afrodesiac*

aplomb, not *aplom*

apocryphal, not *apocriphal*

apostle, not *apostal*

apostrophe, not *apostraphe*

apparent, not *apparant*

apropos, not *appropos*

aquarium, not *aquareum*

Aquarius, not *Acquarius*

archaeology, not *archiology*

arctic, not *artic*

argument, not *arguement*

arid, not *airid*

arithmetic, not *arithmatic*

arraign, not *arrain*

arsenic, not *arsnic*

arthritis, not *artheritis*

article, not *artical*

artifact, not *artifack*

artistically, not *artisticly*

ascertain, not *ascertane*

ascetic, not *assetic*

asinine, not *assinine*

asparagus, not *asparigus*

aspect, not *aspeck*

aspirin, not *asprin*

assassin, not *asassin*

assistant, not *assistent*

asterisk, not *astarisk*

asthma, not *azthma*

atheist, not *athiest*

athletic, not *atheletic*

atonement, not *attonement*

attempt, not *attemp*

attendance, not *attendence*

attorney, not *attorny*

audible, not *audable*

auxiliary, not *auxilary*

avalanche, not *avalanch*

average, not *avarage*

avocado, not *avacado*

avoidable, not *avoidible*

awfully, not *awefully*

axle, not *axel*

ayatollah, not *ayatolah*

B

babbling, not *babling*

Babylonian, not *Babilonian*

baboon, not *babboon*

baccalaureate, not *bacallaureate*

bacchanalian, not *backanalian*

bachelor, not *batchlor*

bacillus, not *baccilus*

backboard, not *backbord*

backgammon, not *backammon*

backpack, not *backpak*

badminton, not *badmitton*

bagel, not *bagle*

bailiff, not *baillif*

ballad, not *balad*

ballistic, not *balistic*

balloon, not *baloon*

balsam, not *balsom*

banana, not *bannana*

bandage, not *bandege*

bandit, not *bandet*

banister, not *bannister*

baptize, not *babtize*

baptism, not *babtism*

barbarian, not *barberian*

barbecue, not *barbicue*

barbiturate, not *barbiturite*

bargain, not *bargin*

barnacle, not *barnacal*

baroque, not *beroque*

barracks, not *baracks*

barracuda, not *barricuda*

barrier, not *barrior*

bartender, not *bartendor*

basin, not *basen*

basket, not *baskit*

bastard, not *basterd*

battalion, not *battalian*

bauble, not *bawble*

bayonet, not *bayanet*

bawdy, not *baudy*

bazaar, not *bazarr*

beacon, not *beakon*

beauteous, not *beautious*

beaver, not *beever*

beechnut, not *beachnut*

beginning, not *begining*

beggar, not *begger*

beguile, not *begile*

behemoth, not *behemuth*

beige, not *biege*

believe, not *beleive*

bellicose, not *bellicose*

bellwether, not *bellweather*

benefactor, not *benifactor*

benign, not *benine*

benevolent, not *benivolent*

berserk, not *bersurk*

besiege, not *beseige*
betroth, not *betrothe*
beverage, not *bevarege*
bibliography, not *bibleography*
bicarbonate, not *bicarbenate*
biceps, not *bicepts*
bigamy, not *bigomy*
bigotry, not *bigatry*
billiards, not *biliards*
billionaire, not *billionnaire*
binary, not *binery*
bindery, not *bindary*
biodegradable, not *biodegradible*
biography, not *biogrophy*
bipartisan, not *bipartison*
biorhythm, not *biorythm*
biscuit, not *bisket*
biological, not *bialogical*
bivouac, not *bivwack*
bizarre, not *bizare*
blasphemy, not *blasphamy*
blatant, not *blatent*
blithe, not *blith*
blizzard, not *blizzerd*
blockade, not *blockaid*
bludgeon, not *bludgen*
bodice, not *boddice*
boisterous, not *boistrous*
bologna, not *bolony*
bookkeeper, not *bookeeper*
bosom, not *busom*
boudoir, not *boodoir*
bouillabaisse, not *boulliabaise*
bouquet, not *boquet*
bourgeois, not *bourgois*
boutonniere, not *boutonierre*
brassiere, not *brasier*
brief, not *breif*

bristle, not *brissel*
Britain, not *Brittin*
brocade, not *brocaid*
broccoli, not *brocolli*
brokerage, not *brokrage*
bronchial, not *broncheal*
browse, not *browze*
Brussels sprouts, not *brussle sprouts*
buccaneer, not *bucanneer*
Buddha, not *budda*
bulbous, not *bullbous*
bulletin, not *bulliten*
buoy, not *bouy*
buoyant, not *bouyant*
bureau, not *burreau*
bureaucracy, not *burocracy*
burglar, not *burgler*
bustle, not *bussell*

C

cache, not *cashe*
cadre, not *cadry*
calendar, not *calander*
caliber, not *calaber*
calisthenics, not *calasthenics*
calvary, not *calvery*
camaraderie, not *camraderie*
camouflage, not *camaflage*
candidate, not *candadate*
cantaloupe, not *cantalope*
capable, not *capabel*
cappuccino, not *cappaccino*
caravan, not *carivan*
cardiovascular, not *cardiovasculer*
carnivore, not *carnavore*
carouse, not *carrouse*
carriage, not *carraige*

cashmere, not *cashmeer*

casserole, not *caserole*

cataclysm, not *cateclysm*

catechism, not *catichism*

category, not *catagory*

caterpillar, not *catapillar*

cathedral, not *cathedrel*

cauliflower, not *calliflower*

caulk, not *cawk*

cavalry, not *calvery*

caveat, not *caviat*

ceiling, not *cieling*

celebrate, not *celabrate*

celibate, not *celabate*

cellar, not *celler*

cemetery, not *cemetary*

centennial, not *centenneal*

certificate, not *certifacate*

centrifugal, not *centrifical*

centerpiece, not *centerpeice*

chagrined, not *chagrenned*

chalice, not *chalise*

challenge, not *chalenge*

chamois, not *shammy*

chandelier, not *chandelear*

changeable, not *changable*

chaperone, not *chaparone*

chaplain, not *chaplin*

characteristic, not *charicteristic*

charade, not *cherade*

charisma, not *carisma*

charity, not *charety*

chartreuse, not *chartruse*

chastise, not *chastize*

chauffeur, not *chaufeur*

chenille, not *chenile*

chieftain, not *chieftan*

chisel, not *chisle*

chlorine, not *chlorene*

chlorophyll, not *chloraphyll*

choreography, not *coreography*

cholera, not *chollera*

cholesterol, not *cholestrol*

chow mein, not *chow main*

chronicle, not *chronacle*

cinnamon, not *cinnimon*

circuit, not *circiut*

circumference, not *circumferance*

circumstantial, not *circumstancial*

cirrhosis, not *cirrosis*

clairvoyance, not *clairvoyence*

claustrophobia, not *clostrophobia*

clientele, not *clientell*

coalition, not *colition*

codeine, not *codene*

coincidence, not *coincidance*

cognizant, not *cognizent*

coiffure, not *coifure*

cole slaw, not *coldslaw*

collector, not *collecter*

cologne, not *collogne*

colossal, not *collosal*

column, not *collum*

comfortable, not *comfortible*

commemorate, not *comemmorate*

commissary, not *commisary*

commission, not *commision*

commitment, not *committment*

committed, not *comitted*

committee, not *commitee*

comparative, not *comparitive*

compatible, not *compatable*

competent, not *competant*

competition, not *compatition*

complexion, not *complection*

comprehensible, not *comprehensable*

comptroller, not *comtroller*
concede, not *consede*
conceive, not *concieve*
conceivable, not *conceivible*
condominium, not *condomineum*
consensus, not *concensus*
condemn, not *condemm*
condescend, not *condascend*
confiscate, not *comfiscate*
congratulate, not *congradulate*
Connecticut, not *Conneticut*
conqueror, not *conquerer*
conscientious, not *consciencious*
consequence, not *consiquence*
consistent, not *consistant*
constipation, not *constepation*
constitution, not *constetition*
consultant, not *consultent*
contagious, not *contageous*
contemptible, not *contemptable*
continuance, not *continuence*
controlling, not *controling*
controversial, not *contraversial*
convalescence, not *convelescence*
convenient, not *conveniant*
conversant, not *conversent*
convertible, not *convertable*
coolly, not *cooly*
coquette, not *coquett*
corduroy, not *cordaroy*
corollary, not *corrolary*
correlate, not *corellate*
correspondent, not *correspondant*
corruptible, not *corruptable*
cough, not *coff*
counterfeit, not *conterfit*
courageous, not *couragious*
courteous, not *courtious*

courtesy, not *curtesy*
court-martial, not *court-marshall*
creditable, not *credittible*
criticize, not *critisize*
croissant, not *crossant*
crucifixion, not *crucifiction*
cryptic, not *criptic*
cupboard, not *cubbard*
curmudgeon, not *curmugeon*
curtsy, not *courtsy*
customary, not *custemary*
Czechoslovakia, not *Czechoslavakia*

D

dachshund, not *dachsund*
daiquiri, not *daiquiry*
damage, not *dammage*
damnable, not *dammable*
dandelion, not *dandalion*
dappled, not *dappeled*
dawdle, not *daudle*
deadening, not *deadning*
deactivate, not *deactavate*
dealer, not *dealor*
dearth, not *durth*
debacle, not *debackle*
debonair, not *debanair*
debrief, not *debreif*
debtor, not *debter*
decadence, not *decadance*
decaffeinated, not *decafeinated*
decapitate, not *decapatate*
deceive, not *decieve*
decibel, not *decible*
deciduous, not *desiduous*
decimal, not *decimel*
decrepit, not *decrepet*

deductible, not *deductable*

defamation, not *defimation*

defecate, not *deficate*

defendant, not *defendent*

deferred, not *defered*

defiance, not *defience*

deficit, not *deficet*

defined, not *defind*

definite, not *defanite*

definitely, not *definitly*

deify, not *diafy*

delicatessen, not *delicatesen*

delirious, not *delerious*

demagogue, not *demigogue*

demeanor, not *demeaner*

demographic, not *demagraphic*

demonstrator, not *demonstrater*

denunciation, not *denounciation*

deodorant, not *deoderant*

dependence, not *dependance*

depravity, not *depravaty*

depressant, not *depressent*

deprivation, not *deprevation*

derelict, not *derelick*

descendant, not *decendant*

design, not *desine*

desirable, not *desirible*

despair, not *dispair*

desperately, not *desperitely*

despondent, not *despondant*

develop, not *develope*

deviant, not *devient*

devise, not *devize*

diaphragm, not *diaphram*

diarrhea, not *diarhea*

difference, not *differance*

digestible, not *digestable*

dilemma, not *delimma*

dilettante, not *dilletante*

dimension, not *deminsion*

dinghy, not *dingey*

diphtheria, not *diptheria*

disappear, not *disapear*

disappoint, not *disapoint*

disastrous, not *disasterous*

disciple, not *desciple*

discipline, not *disapline*

disillusion, not *disallusion*

disinfectant, not *disinfectent*

disparaging, not *disperaging*

disparate, not *disperate*

dispel, not *dispell*

dispensable, not *dispensible*

disreputable, not *disreputible*

dissatisfied, not *disatisfied*

dissonant, not *disonant*

dissuade, not *disuade*

distraught, not *distraut*

doctrinaire, not *doctrenaire*

dominant, not *dominent*

dormitory, not *dormatory*

dowry, not *dowery*

drudgery, not *drugery*

drunkenness, not *drunkeness*

dumbbell, not *dumbell*

duress, not *durress*

dyslexia, not *dislexia*

E

eagle, not *eagel*

earnest, not *ernest*

earring, not *earing*

easel, not *easle*

ebullient, not *ebulient*

eccentricity, not *eccentrisity*

eclipse, not *ecclipse*
echoes, not *echos*
ecstasy, not *ecstacy*
eczema, not *egzema*
edible, not *edable*
efficiency, not *efficiancy*
effigy, not *effegy*
effrontery, not *effrontry*
eighth, not *eigth*
elaborate, not *elaberate*
electrically, not *electricly*
electrolysis, not *electrolasis*
elegy, not *eligy*
elementary, not *elementry*
elevator, not *elevater*
eligible, not *eligable*
ellipse, not *elipse*
eloquent, not *elaquent*
elves, not *elfs*
embarrass, not *embarass*
embezzle, not *embezzel*
emblem, not *emblam*
emperor, not *emperer*
encephalitis, not *enceffalitis*
enterprise, not *enterprize*
enthusiastically, not *enthusiasticly*
entrepreneur, not *entreprenuer*
environment, not *envirnment*
ephemeral, not *effemeral*
epiphany, not *epifany*
epistle, not *episle*
epitaph, not *epetaph*
equator, not *equater*
equilibrium, not *equalibrium*
equipped, not *equipt*
equivalent, not *equivelant*
erroneous, not *erronious*
esophagus, not *esophogus*

especially, not *especilly*
espresso, not *expresso*
estuary, not *estuery*
ethyl, not *ethel*
etiquette, not *etiquit*
euphemism, not *euphamism*
euthanasia, not *euthenasia*
evolution, not *evalution*
exaggerate, not *exagerate*
exasperate, not *exasparate*
exceed, not *exeed*
excel, not *exell*
excellence, not *excellance*
excerpt, not *excerp*
exhaust, not *exaust*
exhilarate, not *exhillerate*
exhume, not *exume*
existence, not *existance*
expectorant, not *expectorent*
expendable, not *expendible*
expense, not *expence*
explanation, not *explenation*
exponent, not *exponant*
extraordinary, not *extrordinary*
extrapolate, not *extrapellate*
extravagant, not *extravogant*
extricate, not *extracate*
exuberance, not *exuberence*

F

facetious, not *faceteous*
facsimiles, not *faxsimiles*
Fahrenheit, not *Farenheit*
fallacious, not *fallaceous*
fallacy, not *fallecy*
familiar, not *familier*
farcical, not *farsical*

farewell, not *fairwell*

fascinate, not *fasinate*

fateful, not *fatefull*

fathom, not *fathem*

fatigue, not *fetigue*

favor, not *faver*

feasible, not *feasibel*

February, not *Febuary*

felicitous, not *falicitous*

fiancé, not *feancé*

fiancée, not *feancée*

fictitious, not *fictiteous*

fiftieth, not *fiftyeth*

figment, not *figament*

finicky, not *finacky*

financially, not *financialy*

financier, not *financior*

flourish, not *florish*

flotation, not *floatation*

fluency, not *fluancy*

fluorescent, not *fluoresent*

foliage, not *folage*

forbearance, not *forebearance*

forbidding, not *forebidding*

forcibly, not *forceably*

forearm, not *forarm*

foreboding, not *forboding*

forecast, not *forcast*

foreclosure, not *forclosure*

forehead, not *forhead*

foreign, not *forein*

foresee, not *forsee*

forfeit, not *forfiet*

formaldehyde, not *formaldehide*

formidable, not *formidible*

forty, not *fourty*

forward, not *forword*

foreword, not *foreward*

fragile, not *fragil*

freight, not *fraight*

Freudian, not *Freudien*

frightening, not *frightning*

fuchsia, not *fushia*

fulfill, not *fullfill*

fundamentally, not *fundamently*

furlough, not *furlow*

fuselage, not *fusilage*

G

gable, not *gabel*

gaiety, not *gaety*

gale, not *gail*

galoshes, not *galloshes*

galvanize, not *galvenize*

gambit, not *gambet*

garrulous, not *garralous*

gauge, not *guage*

genealogy, not *geneology*

genius, not *geneus*

geology, not *gealogy*

geyser, not *guyser*

ghastly, not *gastly*

ghetto, not *getto*

gingham, not *gingam*

glacier, not *glasier*

glaucoma, not *glocoma*

gonorrhea, not *gonorhea*

government, not *goverment*

governor, not *governer*

grammar, not *grammer*

grease, not *greese*

grenadine, not *grenedine*

grievous, not *grievious*

guarantee, not *gaurantee*

guess, not *gess*

guest, not *gest*
guerrilla, not *guerilla*
guidance, not *guidence*
gynecology, not *gynocology*

H

handkerchief, not *hankerchief*
handyman, not *handiman*
happily, not *hapilly*
harangue, not *harang*
harass, not *harrass*
harlequin, not *harliquin*
harpsichord, not *harpsicord*
height, not *hieght*
heinous, not *hainous*
heir, not *hier*
hemorrhage, not *hemorhage*
hemorrhoid, not *hemorhoid*
heroes, not *heros*
hesitancy, not *hesitency*
hierarchy, not *hirearchy*
hieroglyphics, not *hierogliphics*
hindrance, not *hindrence*
hoarse, not *hoarce*
hollandaise, not *hollandaze*
holocaust, not *holocost*
hors d'oeuvre, not *hor d'oevre*
humorous, not *humerous*
hyena, not *hyina*
hygiene, not *hygeine*
hype, not *hipe*
hyperbole, not *hyperboll*
hypnotize, not *hypnatize*
hypocrisy, not *hypocracy*
hypothesis, not *hypothosis*
hysteria, not *hystaria*
hysterectomy, not *histerectomy*

I

icicle, not *icecycle*
iconoclast, not *iconaclast*
idealize, not *idealise*
ideally, not *idealy*
ideology, not *idealogy*
idiom, not *idium*
idiosyncrasy, not *ideosyncrasy*
idle, not *idel*
idol, not *idole*
idolatry, not *idolitry*
idyllic, not *idylic*
ignoble, not *ignobel*
ignorance, not *ignorence*
iguana, not *iguanna*
illegal, not *illegale*
illiterate, not *illitarate*
imaginary, not *imaginery*
immediate, not *imediate*
implement, not *impliment*
incandescent, not *incandesent*
incidentally, not *incidently*
incite, not *insite*
independence, not *independance*
independent, not *independant*
indict, not *indight*
indispensable, not *indispensible*
inevitable, not *inevatible*
infinitesimal, not *infinitesmal*
influential, not *influencial*
inoculate, not *innoculate*
intercede, not *interceed*
interrupt, not *interupt*
iridescent, not *iradescent*
irrelevant, not *irrelevent*
irresistible, not *irrisistable*
isthmus, not *istmus*

itinerary, not *itinerery*

J

jackal, not *jackle*
jackknife, not *jacknife*
jaguar, not *jagaur*
jai alai, not *jai lai*
jaundice, not *jaundise*
javelin, not *javalin*
jealousy, not *jelousy*
jeopardy, not *jepardy*
jettison, not *jettason*
jewelry, not *jewelery*
jocund, not *jokund*
jonquil, not *johnquil*
jostle, not *jossel*
jubilation, not *jubalation*
judgment, not *judgement*
julienne, not *julianne*
juvenile, not *juvenil*

K

kernel, not *kernal*
knickknack, not *knicknack*
nicknack, not *nicnack*
knowledgeable, not
  knowledgable
khaki, not *kakhi*
kohlrabi, not *kolrabi*
kudos, not *kudoes*
kumquat, not *kumkuat*

L

laboratory, not *labratory*
labyrinth, not *labrinth*

lackadaisical, not
  lackadasical
lacquer, not *laquer*
languorous, not *langorous*
laryngitis, not *larengitis*
larynx, not *larinx*
lascivious, not *lasivious*
laugh, not *luagh*
league, not *leage*
legitimate, not *ligitamate*
leisure, not *liesure*
length, not *lenth*
lenient, not *leniant*
leukemia, not *lukemia*
liaison, not *laiason*
library, not *liberry*
license, not *licence*
licorice, not *licorish*
lieutenant, not *leutenant*
likelihood, not *likelyhood*
limousine, not *limosine*
lineament, not *linament*
literature, not *literture*
logarithm, not *logrythm*
loge, not *loage*
loneliness, not *lonliness*
lonely, not *lonly*
longitude, not *longatude*
luminescent, not *luminesent*
lunacy, not *lunicy*
luscious, not *lushous*
lying, not *lyeing*

M

mackerel, not *mackeral*
mademoiselle, not *mademoselle*
Madeira, not *Madiera*

magazine, not *magasine*

mahogany, not *mahogony*

maintenance, not *maintnance*

maladroit, not *maledroit*

malaise, not *malaize*

malfeasance, not *malfeasence*

malign, not *maline*

malleable, not *malliable*

manageable, not *managable*

maneuver, not *manuver*

manicotti, not *manacotti*

manual, not *manuel*

maraschino, not *marashino*

marriage, not *marraige*

masseur, not *massuer*

masseuse, not *massuese*

mathematics, not *mathmatics*

mattress, not *matress*

mausoleum, not *mausolium*

mayonnaise, not *mayonaise*

measles, not *measels*

Mediterranean, not *Mediteranean*

melancholy, not *melencholy*

memento, not *momento*

mercenary, not *mercernary*

meteorology, not *meterology*

mezzanine, not *mezanine*

millennium, not *millenium*

milquetoast, not *milktoast*

miniature, not *minature*

minuscule, not *miniscule*

minutes, not *minnets*

miscellaneous, not *miscelaneous*

mischief, not *mischef*

mischievous, not *mischivous*

misogynist, not *misogenist*

missile, not *missille*

missionary, not *missionery*

misspell, not *mispell*

misstate, not *mistate*

mnemonic, not *nemonic*

molasses, not *molassis*

monsieur, not *monseur*

moratorium, not *moritorium*

mortarboard, not *morterboard*

mortgage, not *morgage*

mosquitoes, not *mosquitos*

multifarious, not *multiferious*

murmur, not *murmer*

muscle, not *mussle*

mysterious, not *mystereous*

N

narcissism, not *narcisism*

narrative, not *narative*

nauseous, not *nausious*

necessary, not *necesarry*

neighbor, not *nieghbor*

neurosis, not *nuerosis*

neuter, not *nueter*

neutron, not *nuetron*

niece, not *neice*

nihilism, not *nialism*

ninety, not *ninty*

nondescript, not *nondiscript*

noticeable, not *noticable*

nougat, not *nouget*

nuisance, not *nuisence*

nugget, not *nugett*

nymph, not *nynph*

O

obedience, not *obediance*

obeisance, not *obiesance*

obsequious, not *obsequius*
obsolescent, not *obsolesent*
obstacle, not *obstical*
occasion, not *ocassion*
occur, not *ocurr*
occurrence, not *occurence*
occurred, not *occured*
occurring, not *occuring*
o'clock, not *oclock*
odorous, not *odorus*
odyssey, not *odysey*
Oedipus, not *Oedapus*
offense, not *offents*
oligarchy, not *olagarchy*
ombudsman, not *ombusman*
omission, not *ommision*
omitted, not *ommited*
omnipotent, not *omnipatent*
onomatopoeia, not *onomatopia*
ophthalmology, not *opthalmology*
opinion, not *opinnion*
orangutan, not *orangutang*
outrageous, not *outragious*

P

panicky, not *paniky*
paradigm, not *paradime*
parallel, not *paralell*
paranoia, not *paranoea*
paraphernalia, not *paraphenalia*
parliament, not *parlament*
pastime, not *pasttime*
pavilion, not *pavilian*
peaceable, not *peacable*
peculiar, not *peculier*
penguin, not *penquin*
penicillin, not *pennicilin*

penitentiary, not *penitentery*
perceive, not *percieve*
periphery, not *perifery*
permissible, not *permissable*
perseverance, not *perserverance*
persistence, not *persistance*
pestilence, not *pestilance*
phenomenon, not *phenominon*
phlegm, not *phlem*
phlegmatic, not *phlematic*
phosphorescent, not *phospherescent*
physician, not *physicion*
picayune, not *pikayune*
picnicking, not *picnicing*
piece, not *peice*
pigeon, not *pidgin*
pilgrimage, not *pilgrimege*
pitiful, not *pitifull*
plaid, not *plad*
playwright, not *playwrite*
pleasant, not *pleasent*
pneumonia, not *pnuemonia*
poinsettia, not *poinsetta*
politically, not *politicly*
politicking, not *politiking*
Polynesian, not *Polynesean*
pomegranate, not *pomegranet*
porcelain, not *porcelin*
porpoise, not *porpose*
portrait, not *protret*
possess, not *posess*
potatoes, not *potatos*
potpourri, not *popourri*
practically, not *practicly*
prairie, not *prarie*
precede, not *preceed*
preceding, not *preceeding*
preference, not *preferance*

preferred, not *preffered*

prejudice, not *prejudise*

prevalent, not *prevelant*

primeval, not *primevil*

privilege, not *privalege*

probably, not *probabally*

proceed, not *procede*

professor, not *proffesor*

prominent, not *promanent*

pronunciation, not *pronounciation*

propaganda, not *propiganda*

pseudonym, not *psuedonym*

psoriasis, not *soriasis*

psychiatry, not *psychietry*

psychology, not *psycholegy*

pterodactyl, not *terodactyl*

ptomaine, not *tomaine*

pueblo, not *peublo*

Q

quagmire, not *quagmier*

quandary, not *quandry*

quarantine, not *quarentine*

quarry, not *quorry*

quarter, not *quartor*

quench, not *quinch*

query, not *querie*

quesadilla, not *quesedilla*

quiescent, not *quiesent*

questionnaire, not *questionaire*

queue, not *que*

quiche, not *quishe*

quiet, not *quiat*

quintessential, not *quintesential*

quirk, not *querk*

quixotic, not *quihotic*

quizzes, not *quizes*

quorum, not *quorem*

quotable, not *quoteable*

R

rabble, not *rabbel*

raconteur, not *racontuer*

racquet, not *raquet*

rapport, not *raport*

rapprochement, not *rapprochment*

raspberry, not *razzberry*

ravenous, not *ravinous*

realistically, not *realisticly*

realize, not *realise*

recede, not *receed*

receipt, not *receit*

receive, not *receave*

recess, not *resess*

recognize, not *reconize*

recommend, not *recomend*

reconnaissance, not *reconnaisance*

recurrence, not *reocurrence*

reference, not *referance*

referred, not *refered*

reggae, not *reggay*

relevant, not *relavent*

relieved, not *releived*

religious, not *religeous*

religion, not *religeon*

religious, not *religeous*

reminisce, not *reminiss*

reminiscence, not *reminisence*

remittance, not *remitance*

renaissance, not *renaisance*

rendezvous, not *rendevous*

repellent, not *repelant*

repentance, not *repentence*

rescind, not *resind*

reservoir, not *reservor*

restaurant, not *restarant*

resuscitator, not *resussitator*

reverence, not *reverance*

rhapsody, not *rapsody*

rhetorical, not *retorical*

rheumatic, not *reumatic*

rheumatism, not *reumatism*

rhinoceros, not *rinoceros*

rhododendron, not
     rhododendrom

rhyme, not *ryme*

rhythm, not *rhythem*

ridiculous, not *ridiculus*

roommate, not *roomate*

S

sabbatical, not *sabatical*

saccharine, not *saccarine*

sacrilege, not *sacrilage*

sacrilegious, not *sacrilegeous*

samurai, not *samarai*

sandwich, not *sanwich*

sanguine, not *sanguin*

sapphire, not *saphire*

sarcophagus, not *sarcophigus*

sarsaparilla, not *sasparilla*

satellite, not *satelite*

satin, not *saten*

satire, not *satier*

satyr, not *sater*

sauerkraut, not *sourkraut*

scary, not *scarey*

scenario, not *sceenario*

scenery, not *scenary*

scepter, not *septor*

schedule, not *scedule*

schizophrenia, not *schizaphrenia*

schnauzer, not *schnowzer*

schooner, not *scooner*

scintillate, not *sintillate*

scissors, not *scisors*

scythe, not *scyth*

secede, not *seceed*

secession, not *sesession*

secretary, not *secretery*

seismology, not *siesmology*

seize, not *sieze*

seminary, not *seminery*

sentence, not *sentense*

separate, not *seperate*

separately, not *seperately*

sequoia, not *sequoea*

sergeant, not *sargeant*

sesame, not *sesamee*

shepherd, not *sheperd*

shelves, not *shelfs*

sheriff, not *sherrif*

shoo-in, not *shoe-in*

siege, not *seige*

sieve, not *seive*

silhouette, not *silouette*

similar, not *simular*

simile, not *similee*

sincerely, not *sincerly*

skeptical, not *sceptical*

skiing, not *skeing*

soliloquy, not *solliloquy*

somersault, not *somersalt*

sophomore, not *sophamore*

souvenir, not *souvenire*

spacious, not *spaceous*

specimen, not *specimon*

specious, not *speceous*
spherical, not *sphericle*
sphinx, not *sphinks*
sponsor, not *sponser*
spontaneity, not *spontaniety*
spontaneous, not *spontanious*
squeamish, not *squeemish*
squirrel, not *squirel*
staccato, not *stacato*
stalactite, not *stalagtite*
statuesque, not *statuesk*
straight, not *streight*
strait, not *strate*
stratagem, not *stratigem*
strategy, not *stratigy*
stratosphere, not *stratasphere*
strengthen, not *strenthen*
strenuous, not *strenuos*
streusel, not *streusle*
stubbornness, not *stubborness*
subterranean, not *subteranean*
subtle, not *suttle*
succeed, not *succede*
success, not *sucess*
sufficient, not *sufficiant*
suffrage, not *suffrege*
suit, not *sute*
suite, not *suete*
superintendent, not *superintendant*
supersede, not *superseed*
suppress, not *supress*
surround, not *suround*
surveillance, not *surveilance*
susceptible, not *susceptable*
suspicious, not *suspiceous*
syllable, not *sylable*
symmetrical, not *symetrical*
synagogue, not *synogogue*

syncopation, not *syncapation*
synchronize, not *synchranize*
synonymous, not *synonimous*
syringe, not *syrenge*

T

tachometer, not *tachometre*
tambourine, not *tambarine*
tangible, not *tangable*
tariff, not *tarrif*
technical, not *technicle*
technique, not *techneque*
temperance, not *temperence*
temperature, not *temperture*
tendency, not *tendancy*
tenement, not *tenament*
tensile, not *tensil*
their, not *thier*
theologian, not *theologean*
theories, not *theries*
therapeutic, not *theraputic*
thorough, not *thorow*
though, not *tho*
through, not *thrue*
threshold, not *threshhold*
tirade, not *tiraid*
tobacco, not *tobbaco*
toboggan, not *tobbogan*
tomatoes, not *tomatos*
toreador, not *toriador*
tournament, not *tournamant*
tourniquet, not *tourniquit*
transference, not *transferense*
transcend, not *transend*
trapeze, not *trapeeze*
trellis, not *treliss*
trousseau, not *trouseau*

troubadour, not *troubador*
Tuesday, not *Teusday*
tycoon, not *tycune*
tyranny, not *tyrany*

U

ubiquitous, not *ubiquetous*
ultimatum, not *ultamatum*
ukulele, not *ukalele*
umbilical, not *umbillical*
unanimous, not *unanamous*
unconscionable, not *unconscianable*
undeniable, not *undeniabel*
undoubtedly, not *undoutedly*
unkempt, not *unkemp*
unmentionables, not *unmentionibles*
unnecessary, not *unecessary*
unscrupulous, not *unscrupulus*
unusual, not *unusuel*
upholstery, not *upolstery*
urchin, not *urchan*
urinal, not *urinel*
unnatural, not *unatural*
usage, not *usege*
useful, not *usefull*
usually, not *usualy*
utensil, not *utensal*
uterine, not *uterin*
utilize, not *utilise*
utterance, not *utterence*

V

vaccinate, not *vacinnate*
vacillate, not *vaccilate*
vacuum, not *vacum*
valuable, not *valuble*

vanilla, not *vanella*
variegated, not *varigated*
vehement, not *vehemant*
vengeance, not *vengeanse*
verisimilitude, not *verisimiltude*
vermilion, not *vermillian*
versus, not *versas*
veterinarian, not *veternarian*
vicarious, not *vicareous*
vice versa, not *visa versa*
vicissitude, not *visissitude*
vigilance, not *vigilence*
villain, not *villan*
vinegar, not *vineger*
violence, not *violance*
virtuous, not *virtous*

W

wariness, not *waryness*
warrant, not *warrent*
Wednesday, not *Wensday*
weird, not *wierd*
wholly, not *wholy*
withhold, not *withold*

X

Xanadu, not *Xanidu*
xenophobe, not *xenaphobe*
xerography, not *xerogrophy*
xylophone, not *xylaphone*

Y

yacht, not *yaht*
yarmulke, not *yarmulka*
yeoman, not *yoeman*

yield, not *yeild*
yoke, not *yoak*

Z

zealot, not *zealat*
zephyr, not *zephir*
zoological, not *zological*
zygote, not *zygoat*

Chapter Six

New Words and Phrases

The English have no respect for their language, and will not teach
their children to speak it.

—GEORGE BERNARD SHAW, *PLAYS PLEASANT AND UNPLEASANT*

WHAT GEORGE BERNARD SHAW SAID so many years ago about the English certainly seems to describe present-day Americans as well. We Americans have even less respect for our language than the English do. Throughout our history, we have taken many words as our own from other languages. We consider very few words sacrosanct and we're constantly assigning new meanings to old established words.

We are probably the most creative people in the world when it comes to language. We love to make up words. And we get many of our new words from the younger generation. The current lexicon of words does not suffice to describe our world because it is changing too fast. The technological explosion created a need to invent new words to define the changes. Most adults were not born with computers in their homes. But now computers are nearly as prevalent as television sets and some preschoolers have become adept at using them before they can even read. Very often we find children teaching their parents the new language of technology.

New words and phrases are popping up faster than ever before. It is partly because of all the words and terminology that have been created for computers and the Internet. But a lot have been coined through new forms of music (hip-hop and rap, for example), new scientific and medical discoveries, the media, politics, and psychology. Many older words have taken on new meanings, too. These new words and terms, called neologisms, spread like wildfire because communication is now faster and more widespread than it has ever been. Americans in particular seem to have a propensity to neologize.

The following list contains a few of the words and phrases that have come into being or have acquired an additional meaning during the past few years. These words and phrases have been collected from the Internet, from newspapers and magazines, and from dictionary publishers' lists of new words. I find some of them amusing and include them for that reason alone.

abdominoplasty a surgical operation to remove excess flesh from the abdomen

abibliophobia fear of running out of things to read

aerobicize to tone the body by aerobic exercise

affluenza extreme materialism in which consumers overwork and accumulate enormous debt to purchase more goods

agita a feeling of agitation or anxiety

agony aunt a columnist who writes an advice column

agritourist one who tours agricultural areas to see farms and perhaps to participate in farming activities

agroterrorism terrorist acts involving the disruption, damage, or destruction of a country's agriculture

agroterrorist one who commits

terrorist acts that target agriculture

alcolock an electronic device fitted to the ignition of a car to stop a driver from starting it if the driver has drunk more alcohol than the legal limit for driving

al desko something you do while at your desk: *I usually have lunch al desko while I answer my e-mail.*

alterity otherness; the quality of being radically alien to the conscious self; a particular cultural orientation

anandamide a derivative of arachidonic acid that occurs naturally in the brain and in some foods, such as chocolate, and that binds to the same brain receptors as cannabinoids (the chemical compounds that are the active principles of marijuana)

ape diet a vegetarian diet that

emphasizes soy protein, soluble fiber, nuts, and leafy green vegetables

aquascape   a scenic view of a body of water; an area with an aquatic feature such as a pond or fountain

arm candy   an attractive person: *The mogul is just using that beautiful young thing as arm candy.*

attrit   destroy an enemy with large amounts of troops or firepower; reduce something in size or strength; to wear down by attrition

avatar   an electronic image in a computer game or various online sites

avian flu   influenza carried by birds that is caused by the influenza A virus and can be transmitted to other invertebrates; also called *bird flu*

bad hair day   a disagreeable day in which one's hair looks weird and one feels stupid looking

bahookie   Scottish, a person's buttocks

balls-to-the-wall   unrestrained, aggressive, all-out; at top speed; with maximum effort: *a balls-to-the-wall race*

bandwidth   the range of frequencies or the measured amount of information that can be transmitted over a connection; also used as a measure of a person's ability or lack of it: *He's not good at multitasking; he has low bandwidth.*

barista   a professionally trained person who makes and serves coffee in a coffee bar

best of breed   any animal, item, or product considered the best of its kind

big-box   a large chain store with a boxlike appearance

biodiesel   a fuel similar to diesel that is made from vegetable oil

bindaas   (Indian) carefree, fashionable, and independent-minded; literally, without servitude

binner   a person who collects and sells used bottles and cans that he has found in recycling bins and dumpsters

bissextile   a leap year

blamestorming   a meeting of colleagues at work, trying to decide who to blame for a mistake or failed project that no one is willing to take responsibility for

bleeding edge   technology that is so new that the user will risk problems in order to use it; new and extremely expensive technology; a term formed as an allusion to "leading edge"

bling, also **bling bling**   expensive, gaudy jewelry; a lifestyle of excessive spending and ostentation

blog   short for Web log, a user-generated Web site that provides

commentary on a particular subject

blowback   unintended adverse
results of a political action or situation

bludge   goof off, avoid work;
sponge

bobo   an affluent and successful
person who has a preference for
countercultural ideas

bogart   intimidate; to use without
sharing

bogof   an acronym for *buy one, get
one free*

bogosity   the degree to which a
thing becomes bogus

bogotify   to change something so
that it becomes useless or non-
functional; to counterfeit

boo   a person's boyfriend or girlfriend

bouncebackability   to become
successful after having failed

brandslut   a consumer who has
no loyalty to a particular brand

bridezilla   a bride-to-be who
becomes selfish, greedy, and
obnoxious while planning her
wedding

bright-line   providing an unam-
biguous criterion or guideline

Brokeback marriage   a marriage
in which one partner is gay and
the other is straight

bubble   a booming economy that
could end in a sudden collapse

bubkes, bupkes, bupkus   a very
small amount; nothing

burka, burqa   a loose garment
that covers the face and body

cack-handed   left-handed;
clumsy, awkward

cankle   an ankle that is so thick it
appears to be a continuation of
the calf

cantopop   Cantonese pop music

carbon neutral   emitting no net
carbon dioxide into the atmosphere

cariad   (Welsh) darling, sweet-
heart, love

celebutante   a celebrity who is
well known in fashionable society; a blend of *celebrity* and
debutante

celebutard   a celebrity who is
perceived to be unintelligent; a
blend of *celebutante* and *retard*

chad   a tiny chip of paper left
hanging in hole-punched cards
and ballots

chick flick   a movie that appeals
more to women than to men

chick lit   books written expressly
for girls and women

chillybin   a container to keep
food or drinks cool

chin music   a high inside pitch in
baseball intended to intimidate
the batter

chugger   a person who stands in a
public place and solicits dona-
tions for a charitable
organization; a blend of the
words *charity* and *mugger*

chupacabra   a vicious animal said

to exist in parts of Central America where it attacks animals, especially goats

climate canary an organism or species whose declining health or numbers signal a larger environmental catastrophe to come

clueful well informed

collateral damage injury inflicted on something other than the intended target, such as civilian casualties of a military operation

comb-over longer hair combed over a bald spot

compadre godfather; close friend, buddy

compierge *see* technology butler

convergence the merging of distinct technologies, industries, or devices into a unified whole

coulrophobia fear of clowns

cruciverbalist a person who compiles or solves crossword puzzles

crunk a type of hip-hop or rap music characterized by repeated shouted catch phrases and elements typical of electronic dance music, such as prominent bass; a person who is very excited or full of energy; a blend of *crazy* and *drunk*

cyberphobia an abnormal or illogical fear of computers

cyberslacker one who uses a company's Internet during office hours for personal activities

cyberspace computer networks and bulletin-board systems where communication takes place

dadah illegal drugs

dashboard diner one who eats while driving

dead presidents money in the form of paper bills; U.S. dollars

dead-cat bounce an insignificant brief recovery that occurs after a steep decline

def cool

deke to fake an opponent out of position, as in ice hockey

de minimis lacking significance or importance; so minor it could be disregarded

deshopper one who buys an item intending to return it for a refund; also called *shopgrifter*

deshopping buying and using something with the intention of returning it for a refund

deuced confounded, devilish, damned

dirty bomb a device using conventional explosives to send nuclear material through the air

dog's breakfast a confused mess or mixture

dooced having lost a job because of something you put in an Internet weblog

dot-commer someone who owns or works for an online company

downshifting quitting a high-pressure job to seek a less stressful life

drainchild an innovative idea that drains resources or funds that could be put to more useful purposes; a brainless idea

drama queen an excessively emotional person

dramedy a dramatic production with comedic elements; a blend of the words *comedy* and *drama*

drink the Kool-Aid to become a firm believer in something without any evidence of veracity; to follow a philosophy blindly

drunk-dial to make an embarrassing phone call when drunk

DWB driving while black: *He got a ticket when his only violation was that he was DWB.*

earworm a song that gets stuck in your head; also called *sticky tune*

ED erectile dysfunction (previously referred to as impotent)

egosurfing searching the Internet for one's own name

eighty-six to discard, reject, refuse: *Eighty-six the drunk guy at the bar.*

elephant in the room a major problem or controversial issue that is present but is ignored or not discussed because it is uncomfortable to do so

embed to place a journalist in a military unit

emulsion a fine dispersion of one liquid or pureed food substance into or onto another

energy bar a nutritious high-protein bar

enigmatologist a person who studies and writes word, logic, or mathematical puzzles

enterdrainment entertainment that is so trite and mind numbing that it sucks the intelligence out of the listener or viewer

extended financial family three generations of the same family who live together in one house out of financial necessity

eye candy a beautiful thing or person

fanboy a male fan, especially one who is obsessive about comics, music, or science fiction

fast-track relating to authority granted to the President of the United States by Congress that allows the President to negotiate trade agreements that Congress must confirm or reject in their entirety

fauxhawk a hairstyle in which a strip of hair across the top of the head is longer and higher than the hair on the sides

fen-phen a former drug combination of phentermine with either fenfluramine or dexfenfluramine; also called *phen-fen*

flash mob a large group of people who gather in a predetermined place to perform some brief action and then disperse

flex dollars discretionary funds used at universities that serve as a form of payment for food, books, etc.

flexitarian one who eats mostly a vegetarian diet but will occasionally eat meat or fish

flog a fake blog that promotes products

Frankenfood genetically engineered food

Freddie Mac a mortgage funder

freegan one who eats food that has been thrown away; one who gathers surplus food that would otherwise be discarded; an anti-consumerist

freeganism a political philosophy that opposes over-consumption and waste

full monty everything; the whole lot

funplex entertainment complex that includes facilities for various sports and games, and often restaurants

gay bomb a chemical weapon that makes enemy soldiers sexually irresistible to each other; also called *love bomb*

gaydar gay radar, the ability to recognize that a person is gay

geek, also **computer geek** an expert in programming and/or repairing computers

gimme cap an adjustable visored cap that often displays a corporate logo or slogan

golden handcuffs special benefits offered to an employee as an inducement to continue service

google to use Google, the Internet search engine, to find information on a person or thing: *She googled her new boyfriend.*

goth music with dark, morbid lyrics; a fan or performer of goth; a person who dresses in black, uses dark dramatic makeup, and often has dyed black hair

granny dumping the abandonment of elderly people in poor health by their relatives or caregivers by leaving them at hospitals or bus depots

greenwash to try to appear environmentally friendly while hiding damaging activities

greige a color between beige and grey; a blend of the words *beige* and *grey*

grief tourist a person who travels specifically to visit a scene of a tragedy or disaster

gripesite a Web site aimed at making consumers aware of deficient goods and services

guyliner eyeliner designed for and used by men

hactivitist someone who writes code or otherwise manipulates bits to promote political ideology such as free speech, human rights, or information ethics; another definition is a person who maliciously undermines the security of the Internet for political purposes

hand-me-up   something a younger person gives to an older person, such as a computer

hardscape   man-made features used in landscape architecture, such as walls or walkways, as contrasted with vegetation

hasbian   a former lesbian who is now in a heterosexual relationship; a blend of *has* and *lesbian*

headbanger   a musician who performs hard rock; a fan of hard rock music

headhunt   to recruit personnel, especially executives, for top-level jobs

healthspan   a period of good health in a person's life

heart-healthy   conducive to a healthy heart and circulatory system: *heart-healthy food; heart-healthy exercise*

himbo   handsome but vacuous male; male bimbo

Hinglish   a blend of *Hindi* and *English*, in particular a variety of English used by speakers of Hindi, characterized by frequent use of Hindi vocabulary or constructions

home shopping   shopping at home from goods displayed on TV shopping channels or on the Web

hoody or hoodie   a person, especially a child, wearing a hooded top

hospitalist   a physician who specializes in treating hospital patients

identity theft   when someone wrongfully obtains and uses another person's personal data such as a social security number to obtain money or   credit

infomania   a condition of reduced concentration caused by continually responding to e-mail, text-messaging, etc.

infomercial   a half-hour or hour-long television commercial

intranet   a computer network with restricted access; often used within a corporation using software and protocols developed for the Internet

irritable male syndrome   anger and bad temper in men caused by a sudden drop in testosterone levels, particularly when brought on by stress

judder bar   a speed bump

junk DNA   a region of DNA that usually consists of a repeating DNA sequence, does not code for protein, and has no known function

label mate   a singer or musician signed to the same record company as another

labradoodle   a cross between a Labrador retriever and a poodle

keypad a section on a computer keyboard that groups together numeric keys; a similar type of panel used in conjunction with a TV set or other electronic device

keypal an e-mail pen pal

killer app a computer application that is so popular that it assures the success of the technology with which it is associated; a feature or component that in itself makes something worth having

king kong a very loud car stereo system

longneck beer served in a long-necked bottle

lookism or **looksism** prejudice or discrimination based on physical appearance, especially that which is considered to fall short of societal notions of beauty

low-hanging fruit easiest task; most readily achievable goal

lurk to read messages on an Internet discussion forum without contributing information

MacGuffin or **McGuffin** an object, event, or character in a story that lacks intrinsic importance but serves to set and keep the plot in motion

McJob a low-paying, dead-end job, such as at a fast-food restaurant

magalogue a catalog that resembles a magazine

man cave an area of a house, such as a basement, workshop, or garage where a man can be alone with his power tools and projects

manga Japanese comic book or graphic novel

marble ceiling a barrier that discriminates by keeping certain classes of people out of the upper echelon of American government, as opposed to *glass ceiling* because at least one can see through a glass ceiling

marriage lite a relationship similar to marriage but without legal implications; civil union concept; living together

mentee a person who is counseled or trained by a mentor

mesotherapy a procedure in which pharmaceuticals, vitamins, or other substances are injected into the mesodermal layer of tissue under the skin to promote the loss of cellulite

me time a period set aside by a person to relax and do something he or she really enjoys

metrosexual a young, straight, sensitive urban male who enjoys good clothes, stylish living, the art of decorating, and self-improvement

middle youth a person between 30 and 45 who doesn't want to be considered middle-aged

Mirandize   to read the Miranda rights to a person under arrest

miswanting   wanting something you mistakenly think will give you pleasure or be fulfilling

mitumba   (eastern and central Africa) secondhand clothing, especially that donated by aid agencies in the West

molecular gastronomy   the application of scientific principles to the understanding and development of food preparation

moshing   frenzied dancing characterized by jumping about, pushing and shoving others to music, particularly loud punk rock, hardcore, or heavy metal music

mosh pit   an area in front of a stage where very physical and rough dancing takes place at a rock concert

mouse potato   an intensive computer user; one who spends a lot of time at the computer

muggle   a person lacking a skill; an unimaginative adult who doesn't understand children; slang for marijuana, coined by jazz musicians in the 1920s and 1930s

murse   a man's purse

my bad   my mistake, my fault

mzee   (in East Africa) an older person; an elder; an ancestor

nanopublishing   low-cost online publishing which incorporates techniques used in writing weblogs to target a specific audience

nanoscale   having dimensions measured in nanometers

nanotube   a carbon molecule that resembles a chicken wire-linked cylinder

navel-gazing   useless or excessive self-contemplation

nimby or NIMBY   acronym for *not in my back yard*; opposition to something offensive or hazardous nearby

noughties   a humorous name for the decade from 2000 to 2009, in imitation of the names of other decades, *twenties*, *thirties*, *forties*, etc.

nouse   a computer's pointing mechanism that is steered by moving one's nose; a blend of *nose* and *mouse*

nutraceutical   food that supposedly contains healing properties or other health benefits

obesogenic   something that can cause a person to become excessively fat

offshoring   basing a company's operations overseas to take advantage of lower costs

ollie   a skateboard maneuver in which the skateboarder snaps the board up off the ground; named for Alan Gelfand, a skateboarder whose nickname is Ollie

opportunivore a person who eats food that has been discarded or left unfinished

orthorexia extreme obsession with eating natural and/or healthy foods

overdog a business owner or manager; the person in charge

oy an interjection used to express annoyance, disappointment, or dismay: *Oy, what a job!*

papaphobia fear of the Pope

paralympian a person with physical disabilities who competes in an international sports event

peedie (Scottish) little, small

peloton main body of riders in a bicycle race

personal shopper a person who helps individuals select merchandise

pescetarian a vegetarian who also eats fish

phat highly attractive; desirable; excellent

phishing a scam of sending e-mails from a fake Web site to illegally obtain password information

phreaker a person who breaks into and/or illegally uses a telephone system

picturize adapt a book or script into a film or television show

plagiarhythm downloading tunes or lyrics from the Internet and using them in new songs

plank (British) a stupid person

pluto demote or devalue a person or thing; a pluto (not capitalized) is someone or something that has lost its status (On August 24, 2006, the International Astronomical Union, which decides the official names of all celestial bodies, stated that Pluto was not a true planet because it's "too small and doesn't dominate its neighborhood." They dubbed Pluto a dwarf planet. This means that there are now only eight planets in the solar system.)

podcast digital recording of a broadcast, made available on the Internet

polyamorist a person who has more than one open romantic relationship at a time

polypill a pill combining aspirin, folic acid, and other drugs to reduce heart attacks and strokes

ponzu (Japanese cookery) a sauce or dip made with soy sauce and citrus juice

potscaping decorating with plants in pots; creating a garden with many plants in pots

psyops military operations aimed at influencing the enemy state of mind through noncombative means, such as distribution of leaflets

protiring leaving a stressful or dull job to pursue more interesting and satisfying work

punditocracy a group of powerful and influential political commentators

push poll political telemarketing masquerading as a poll but no one is collecting information or analyzing data and it does not include any demographic questions

qwerty using an older system or product when a newer one would be better (derived from the arrangement of typewriter keys)

radge (Scottish) a wild, crazy, or violent person

regift a gift that was given to one person who then gave it to another

regifting giving something received as a gift to someone else; passing on unwanted gifts

rendition the practice of sending a foreign criminal or terrorist suspect to be covertly interrogated in a country that has less stringent regulations regarding the humane treatment of prisoners

retail politics a style of political campaigning in which the candidate attends local events to target voters on a small-scale or individual basis

retrosexual heterosexual male who does not spend a lot of time on his appearance and lifestyle;

he uses tools and can fix things; he has old-fashioned graces such as opening doors for women; the opposite of metrosexual

riffage informal guitar riffs, especially in rock music

ringtone the sound on a cell phone that signals an incoming call

roofie Rohypnol, a brand name for a very potent tranquilizer producing a sedative effect, amnesia, and muscle relaxation; sometimes used as a date-rape drug

rumint combination of *rumor* and *intelligence;* information from unreliable sources, based on rumors not facts

sandwich generation a generation of people who have to care for their aging parents while still supporting their own children

SERM selective estrogen receptor modulator, a type of drug

sheeple people who tend to follow the crowd; a blend of *sheep* and *people*

shootaround informal basketball practice

shopaholic one who is obsessed with shopping

shopgrifting buying an item to use with the intention of returning it to get a full refund

shovelware content from an existing medium such as a newspaper or book that has been dumped wholesale into another medium, such as the Web

SIPP (in the UK) a self-invested personal pension, a pension plan that enables the holder to choose and manage the investments made

sky surfing parachuting from an airplane with a board attached to one's feet

smashmouth characterized by brute force without finesse

soul patch a small beard under a man's lower lip

spam a disruptive message posted on a computer network; to send spam

speed-dating a way of meeting by talking briefly to several potential romantic partners at an organized event

spim similar to spam but it attacks users through instant messaging

spin a particular viewpoint or bias, especially in the media; slant: *put one's own spin on a news story*

spoiler information about a film, book, or TV show that spoils the enjoyment for someone who has not yet seen it

spyware unauthorized software installed on a computer without the user's knowledge that transmits information about the Internet activities of the user

studentification social and envi-ronmental changes caused by large numbers of students living in particular areas

supersize larger than average or standard sizes; huge; to greatly increase size, amount, or extent of

support customer service, as in tech support

swagger jacker a person who steals someone else's style, lines, jokes, or swagger, passing them off as his own

tankini a woman's two-piece swimsuit consisting of bikini briefs and a tank top

technology butler a hotel staffer who performs technical tasks for hotel guests with computer problems and needs; also called a *compierge* (a blend of *computer* and *concierge*)

technosexual a narcissist who loves his urban lifestyle and tech-nological gadgets; one who has a fondness for computers, cell phones, PDAs, etc.; a metrosex-ual with strong interests in technology

therapize to subject a person to psychological therapy: *don't ther-apize your friends*

tmesis separation of a word into parts by inserting a word in the middle: *abso-blooming-lutely*

toxic bachelor an unmarried man who is selfish, self-centered, insensitive, and afraid of com-mitment

trance   electronic music with a hypnotic quality

tri-band   (of a mobile phone) having three frequencies so that it can be used in different regions

trifecta   three major achievements in various fields; in horse racing: winning first, second, and third place in the correct order

trolleys or **trollies**   (British) underpants or knickers

tweaker   methamphetamine addict

tweener   a player who has some but not all of the necessary characteristics for each of two or more positions, as in football or basketball

twonk   (British) a stupid or foolish person

ubersexual   a confident and compassionate male heterosexual who has a strong interest in good causes

unibrow   eyebrows that grow together and appear to be one long eyebrow across the forehead

upskilling   teaching or learning additional skills

V-chip   a feature of television receivers that allows the blocking of programs based on ratings categories

vermiculture   the cultivation of bloodworms, earthworms, etc., for use as bait or in composting

voice lift   surgical procedure on the vocal cords to make some-

one's voice sound younger

vortal   vertical industry portal; a Web site that provides information and resources for a particular industry

waitron   a waitperson with a machinelike attitude

wakeboarding   riding on a wide board in the wake of the speedboat one is being pulled by

Webmaster   one who designs and maintains a Web site

wedge issue   a very divisive political issue used for drawing voters away from an opposing party whose supporters have conflicting opinions on it

wetware   the human brain, considered functionally similar to computer hardware or software

wheatgrass   a genus of perennial grasses that are important pasture, hay, or turf grasses

wiki   a Web site or database developed by a community of users, allowing any user to add and edit content

yebo   (South African) an exclamation used to show agreement or approval; yes

yogalates   a fitness routine combining the postures and breathing techniques of yoga with Pilates exercises; a blend of *yoga* and *Pilates*

zombie   a computer controlled by a hacker, without the owner's

knowledge, so that it sends large
quantities of data to a Web site,
making it inaccessible to other
users

Index

Most of the words in the index are from the chapter on misused words. Because the first word in each group is already in alphabetical order, that word is not listed in the index. However, since some of the words that are confused with them aren't easy to locate, they are listed here alphabetically with the page number on which they can be found.

Like many writers, MARY EMBREE has had a varied career. During the 1970s and '80s, she worked for television production companies in various capacities. Starting out in sitcoms such as *Good Times*, *One Day at a Time*, and *Three's Company* as assistant to the producer, she later worked as a researcher and writer for Ralph Edwards' *This is Your Life*, a series whose revival in the 1980s lasted only one season. Because times and tastes change, a job in TV is always temporary. So in between TV series, she freelanced as a writer and researcher for TV pilots, and wrote and directed a video documentary for the California Youth Authority.

It wasn't until 1990 when she moved to Ventura, a beach town about an hour north of Los Angeles, that she began writing in earnest. She started with magazine articles and was delighted to find that many of them got published. After editing manuscripts for authors whose books were subsequently published, she decided to try her hand at writing a book herself. Her first book, *A Woman's Way: Stop-Smoking Book for Women*, attracted an agent who sold it to a publisher before she had completed it. Her latest works are *The Author's Toolkit: a Step-by-Step Guide to Writing and Publishing Your Book*, and this book, *The Birds and Bees of Words*. *The Author's Toolkit* was a Writer's Digest Book Club selection in 2003 and received positive reviews in *Library Journal and Los Angeles Times*, among others.

Mary is the founder of two nonprofit literary organizations. Small Publishers, Artists, and Writers Network (SPAWN) was founded in 1997 and provides education, resources, and networking for people in the book industry both in the United States and abroad. The Literary Arts Society of Ventura County (LASVC), for which she also serves as executive director, was incorporated in 2006. It produces the annual Ventura Book Festival and provides ongoing writing programs for youth.